INVOKE THE GODDESS

Visualizations of Hindu, Greek & Egyptian Deities

WHEN IT'S TIME TO LET GO

Are you having trouble ending a relationship? Are you holding on to a certain someone even though you know this is holding you back? One of the many powerful visualizations in *Invoke the Goddess* shows you how to call upon Radha, the Hindu goddess, to help you take the steps to sever the ties that keep you bound.

Begin by visualizing yourself surrounded by a deep blue light. Then, imagine the blue light fading hue by hue into brilliant white.

Holding the bonds you wish to break in your mind's eye, visualize yourself in search of Radha. Let your hurt, grief, and disappointment surface; do not be afraid to feel the sorrow which is natural to this final "goodbye" to your former dreams.

Seek Radha out. She will understand your predicament without explanation, but feel free to explain if it will help clarify matters in your own mind. Hold out to her the cords you wish to break and take three extremely deep inhalations and exhalations. Then watch as Radha raises her silver cleaver and brings it down at your solar plexus. She is so quick and efficient that there is no mess, and the cords snap neatly back into you. Somewhere else, the other person's cords are doing the same thing.

Feel how many new directions you are free to move in. Know that the past cannot be taken from you, but that the future is all your own. Allow Radha to bestow on you some of her pure silver-white light. Breathe the silver in and out and become accustomed to the new sensation of cleanliness and liberation around the bottom of your ribcage. Now that you feel relaxed and refreshed, return to your everyday life. Cocoon yourself in Radha's silver aura whenever you need a psychic shower.

About the Author

Kala Trobe (England) holds an Honors degree in English Literature and manages an antiquarian bookshop in England. She has traveled extensively and visited many of the world's sacred sites. Her experience includes working as a professional Tarot reader, medium, and vocational healer.

To Write to the Author

If you wish to contact the author or would like more information about this book, please write to the author in care of Llewellyn Worldwide and we will forward your request. Both the author and publisher appreciate hearing from you and learning of your enjoyment of this book and how it has helped you. Llewellyn Worldwide cannot guarantee that every letter written to the author can be answered, but all will be forwarded. Please write to:

Kala Trobe
℅ Llewellyn Worldwide
P.O. Box 64383, Dept. K431-6
St. Paul, MN 55164-0383, U.S.A.

Please enclose a self-addressed stamped envelope for reply, or $1.00 to cover costs. If outside U.S.A., enclose international postal reply coupon.

INVOKE

Visualizations of Hindu,

THE

Greek & Egyptian Deities

GODDESS

KALA TROBE

2000

Llewellyn Publications

St. Paul, Minnesota 55164-0383, U.S.A.

FIRST EDITION
Second Printing, 2000

Book design and editing by Karin Simoneau
Cover art © 2000 by Moon Deer
Cover design by Anne Marie Garrison
Interior art by Kate Thomssen

Library of Congress Cataloging-in-Publication Data
Trobe, Kala, 1969-
    Invoke the goddess : visualizations of Hindu, Greek & Egyptian deities / Kala Trobe.
        p. cm.
    Includes bibliographical references and index.
    ISBN 1-56718-431-6
    1. Magic. 2. Goddesses, Hindu—Miscellanea. 3. Goddesses, Egyptian—Miscellanea. 4. Goddesses, Greek—Miscellanea. I. Title.

BF1623.G63 T76 2000
291.2'114—dc21   00-021145

Llewellyn Publications
A Division of Llewellyn Worldwide, Ltd.
P.O. Box 64383, Dept. K431-6
St. Paul, MN 55164-0383, U.S.A.
www.llewellyn.com

 Printed in the United States of America

With thanks to Beauford, David, Moosk, Sue,
and all who've helped me on the Path,
especially Syd, Steph, Paula, and Amanda.

CONTENTS

INTRODUCTION

HOW TO USE THIS BOOK

Invoke the Goddess is a magickal workbook. It is designed to enable anyone to channel specific archetypal energies that are available to all of us. By linking with these entities and maintaining a strong inner will, it is possible to influence the psychic space in which we exist and, thus, to alter personal circumstance.

With this in mind, five goddesses have been selected from each of three major mythological backgrounds: Hindu, Egyptian, and Greek. The exercises and visualizations allow one to access these deities on a personally interactive as well as a cosmic level. Each goddess offers properties and experiences applicable to our physical, emotional, and spiritual lives.

That positive thought brings positive results is the Hallelujah Chorus of this era, and an underlying principle of this book. However, the visualization processes described within are no mere placebo; the godforms involved are intelligent entities and interaction with them may take place in the imagination, but it is not imaginary. As anyone who has practiced such meditations and projected prayers will confirm, they very soon take on a life of their own, and the results inevitably filter down to the material planes.

Equally real is the effect of these encounters on one's psychology. The visualizations lead the participant into a direct encounter with a powerful archetypal deity, whose symbols and presence will make a profound impression on the subconscious. The idea is to stimulate one's innate capacity for self-healing and self-development. The same applies to the visualizations for specific goals, such as acquiring a long-term partner or attaining prosperity; not only does a seeker appeal to a relevant deity, but one's Higher Self is brought into action.

Also included are exercises designed to help seekers delve (in a controlled situation) into the murkier areas of their psyche and, with the aid of a divinity, bring the conflicting currents to check; or, even better, to harness them as a creative energy source. These qualities are particularly available through the more challenging goddesses such as Kali and Durga. Sometimes it becomes necessary to look into the terrible darkness of our own fears before we can experience a trusting deliverance into the light.

All of these inner journeys are described step-by-step as far as is possible without subjecting the voyager to a contrived experience. Room has been left for personal experiences, while every attempt has been made to aid creative thinking and to provide enough signposts to keep the seeker on the right path.

However, any preset routes are by their nature far from definitive, and seekers are encouraged to use their own judgment and interpret them accordingly. Personal encounters are always more relevant than secondhand knowledge, though the latter can be helpful in guiding us to the right area of the universal psyche. These experiences are, after all, archetypal, and subsequently molded by all who have ever undergone them. Because such a clear subconscious map exists in all of us, it is very safe to use one's intuition in these exercises. In doing so, one is accessing wisdom far greater than that normally made available to us.

At the end of each chapter, Tarot cards relevant to the specific Goddess are noted. These attributions summarize the author's perception of the traits particular to each deity and her mundane archetype, thus underlining the relevant symbolism.

HOW TO PERFORM THE VISUALIZATIONS

There are several ways to approach these visualizations.

Many of the exercises are performed by candlelight and involve meditative states, but this does not necessarily exclude the possibility of visualizing while reading the exercises. I have often had powerful experiences while reading and strongly imagining rituals or magickal techniques. If this is the right way for you to operate, then so be it. A great deal can be achieved on the astral plane while the body remains relatively immobile—a principle that underlines all of these visualizations.

If you prefer not to break your meditation by continually referring to the book, one option is to familiarize yourself with the "route" beforehand. Memorize the major symbols, and capture the essence of the goddess by reading the section describing her personality and functions. Once you have committed the exercise to memory, you should be able to perform it while in a relaxed, meditative state.

The second option is to have a friend read the exercise aloud while you visualize it. This can also be done in group situations, with one person reading and everyone else taking the inner journey. This has the added advantage of enabling participants to exchange experiences and information.

Finally, you can read the exercise onto audiotape, leaving yourself plenty of space to accomplish the various stages of the meditation. This allows you to be absolutely relaxed when the visualization is performed, and to drift off into inner space with no holds barred. A couple of attempts at this will enable you to assess your time requirements at each stage.

Mundane Archetypes

Godforms are intelligent patterns of energy elevated into a prolonged and enhanced existence by the continual input of other beings. Some are the remnants of the atavistic necessities of the species, such as warmth (solar deities) and food (gods of hunting and harvest); others have grown from civilization, such as gods of intellect and artistry. Myth attempts to project inner reality onto a cosmic screen as well as to describe the nature of our arrival at consciousness.

Not only are the gods and goddesses alive on the astral planes and in other dimensions, but they are in our very midst every day of every year. I do not mean courtesy of psychic perception alone, but as psychological archetypes alive in all of us in some shape, form, or mixture; usually, the latter. Studying the character traits of these modern-day priests and priestesses, even in their muted form, will give us valuable insight into the modus operandi of myth and legend, and add to our knowledge of the deities. It is also great fun to witness the old ones wandering through our lives in an often quite blatant manner, and it can provide us with valuable psychotherapeutic clues as to our nature and needs. The idea of nomadic archetypes certainly lends a new slant to the theory of reincarnation in certain cases. It does not, I hasten to add, refute it entirely.

Owing to the relevance of these psychological patterns, I have included for each goddess an approximation of her archetype as alive in Western society today. More and more of the godforms are making themselves known in this manner; the age-old constellations of consciousness are comprehensively spangling our inner space.

Channeling the deities has never been easier, either deliberately or unconsciously. The reader will no doubt recognize the types, which, once identified, can provide a valuable source of information for positive use in situations demanding analysis and healing.

RITUAL BATHS

Ritual baths are an excellent preliminary to any magickal endeavor, creating a suitable atmosphere and relaxing body and mind alike. They range from simple salt baths to elaborate psychic consommés, and a recipe appropriate to the individual goddess is given prior to most of the meditations.

In addition to the herbs and essential oils traditionally used in bathing waters, gemstones may be added to cold water and left for a while to imbue it with their specific qualities. Rose quartz, for example, exudes positive, compassionate properties that are of great use when dealing with hurt feelings and lack of faith. A quantity may be left to soak in water, and the water then poured in the bath in conjunction with rose oil and perhaps some pink solarized water. The person who steps into this bath is unlikely to remain unhappy for long.

Color-treated water is particularly good to use in the ritual bath; it strengthens chakras and aids with visualizing them. Candles around the bath also create a suitable ambience. Their colors may be chosen with a specific aim or chakra area in mind. (See guide to color usage below).

A BRIEF GUIDE TO COLOR USAGE

Red: Strength, determination, passion, sex.

Yellow: Emotional healing, health, prosperity, intellect.

Orange: Vitality, happiness, antidepressive.

Green: New beginnings, balance, growth.

Pale Pink: Comfort, heart-mender.

Dark Pink: Fun, challenge, adventure.

Blue: Calming, inspiring.

Violet: Spirituality, inner vision, psychic development.

Turquoise: Self-defense, both psychic and physical. Attunement to the cosmic will in action.

CHAKRAS

There are many books available on auras and chakras; the amateur reader is advised to purchase one for an invaluable mental map of the psychic bodies. Good examples include the popular *Elements Of . . .* series, published by Penguin Books. For the more advanced reader, Dr. Jonn Mumford's *Chakra and Kundalini Workbook* (Llewellyn, 1995), and Barbara Ann Brennan's *Hands of Light* (Bantam Books, 1987) are recommended. Some books on the subject can be confusing, but it is rare for a book to have absolutely nothing to offer. The problem is exacerbated by the conflict between traditional Hindu-Buddhist symbology and modern interpretations of the chakras. For the sake of clarity, I have adhered to the Westernized version, which allies the chakras with the colors of the spectrum and makes them simple and effective to visualize; however, the arcane symbols and colors are invested with a great deal of energy and may be of more relevance to some readers. It is good to experiment in both schools of thought to find which is best for you. Trial and error is not such a bad method when one's discrimination is constantly exercised.

Chakras, however, are central to the meditation techniques used in this book. The major features of each, modernized but with their basic functions still intact, are outlined here.

The word *chakra* means wheel or discus, and indicates the shape of the energy-points known by that name. These discs of colored light are spiritual and emotional energy-centers to the physical and etheric bodies, and their condition tells much about their owner. They are in some respects the digestive system of the soul, the part of the constitution that takes sustenance from the cosmos and makes it useable to the individual.

As each chakra relates to a separate part of the body and psycho-spiritual function, its speed, depth of color, and condition is indicative of physical, emotional, and spiritual health. For example, a cardiac complaint will be visible in the heart chakra as a rift or murky coloring at the center. Manifestations are as various as their subjects, but, as with the visualizations themselves, certain symbols are universal. A broken heart might manifest as savaged auric fibre or bruised or bloody coloring, while unwillingness to love for fear of rejection may be apparent as an armored area in the chest, or a small tight box.

We see here the root of psychosomatic illness; emotional problems stored in the aura overlap and infect the relevant part of the physical body. The emotional grievance of a broken heart subsequently disrupts the physical health of the body, and can actually bring about a cardiac condition. For those of a sensitive constitution, it is all too easy to literally die of a broken heart—and not just for love; all sorts of disappointments may be responsible. Clearly, the maintenance of a healthy astral body, chakras included, is of paramount importance to total well-being.

Chakras are also the generators of the aura, the glowing body-sheath of energy. By maintaining and conditioning them, we influence every aspect of our manifestation and its well-being.

There are seven major chakras in the human body. They are, in descending order: the crown, third eye, throat, heart, solar plexus, intestinal, and root. Each relates to a particular gland: the pineal, pituitary, thyroid and parathyroid, thymus, pancreas, adrenal, and reproductive, respectively. Each also performs specialized functions, which are indicated below. The Sanskrit name and associated gland are noted in parentheses.

Crown (Sahasrara/Pineal): The crown chakra is located at the center of the top of the skull. It is a major inlet for *prana*, the universal life-energy. This is the chakra most relevant to spiritual matters, and its Sanskrit title translates as "thousand-petalled," the lotus of perfection in meditative symbology. It is an indication of the soul's essential purity that its color is an effulgent white.

Third Eye (Ajna/Pineal/Pituitary): Located between and slightly above the eyebrows in the *bindi* position, this is the center of inner vision, intuition, and innovative ability. Through this chakra we access *Akashic* information, the contents of the "cosmic library" or universal subconscious. Its color is purple.

Throat (Vishuddha/Thyroid): Connected with communication, spiritual guidance, and the ability to listen (and hear), this is an important "people skills" chakra. It is sky-blue and located in the middle back of the throat.

Heart (Anahata/Thymus): This is the green zone in the center of the sternum. Its position allies it to pulmonary as well as cardiac functions. It is strongly associated with the faculty of hope, and is the emotional center regarding love-ties, particularly those of an innocent or aspirational nature.

From the heart chakra extend astral/etheric cords that connect the individual karmically and emotionally to relevant people and places, covering many time-spans. Consequently, it is possible to use these cords to trace, for example, a soul-bonded partner from a former incarnation, or to employ them as telepathic communication cables.

The properties of this chakra are so extensive, covering literally the entire body, that it becomes clear why the proper functioning of the psycho-physical organism requires affection and love, and why the pursuit of it consumes so much of our time on earth.

Solar Plexus (Manipura/Pancreas/Liver): Located a few inches below the heart chakra, in the soft tissue at the bottom of the ribcage, is the yellow solar plexus chakra. This zone is intimately connected with feelings and emotions, and is often the real cause of gastro-intestinal discomfort in times of nervousness and stress, and of gut reactions.

Like the heart chakra, the solar plexus is also a center for telepathic and empathetic communication. The cords that extend from it are representative of one's interaction with other entities, their thickness depending on how frequent the contact has been, and the level of its impact.

Unfortunately, these ties bind us just as tightly to people we hate as to people we love, sometimes more so. There is no better way to build up a lasting psychic rapport with someone than to feel strongly about them, either positively or negatively. Conversely, the best way to avoid being bound with another is to block them from your mind and render them irrelevant from the start. There is more to the advice "turn the other cheek" (i.e., fail to react), than straightforward pacifism. Ignorance really is the best form of defense.

The lines connecting us with people and places of little personal significance are, of course, the thinnest and most difficult to trace.

This center is also connected with morality issues, worldly ambition, and vice.

Intestinal (Swadhisthana/Adrenal): This orange spinning disc is connected with our faculty of interpretation, as well as with digestive and endocrinal functions. Body fluids are controlled from this zone, as are charisma and vitality levels. It therefore affects our ability and desire to interact with others. The intestinal chakra lies halfway down the stomach, between the navel and genitals.

Base (Root/Muladhara/Testes or Ovaries): The red base chakra relates to sexuality and instinctive feelings, such as fear in life-threatening situations. If we have a purely sexual relationship with somebody, they will be connected to us primarily through this chakra. (Although purely sexual relationships are in fact very rare, being more of a function of incomplexity than our constitutions will normally allow.)

The intestinal and base chakras share the function of sustaining our physical response to sex, though all of the chakras have an influence in one way or another on our proper response to psycho-sexual stimuli. The immune system and basic survival modes are also controlled by the root energy center.

MAGICKAL DIET AND EXERCISE

Before appealing to any being on any plane, it is important to have done everything possible to aid one's own cause. If we have not made an effort on our own behalf, why should anybody else bother for us?

Self-maintenance is vitally important on all levels. It helps us to function psychically and magickally if we are in peak physical and mental condition. This means keeping the aura clean, the chakras well oiled, and stress under control. It also demands attention to what we eat and how we live.

There are no hard-and-fast rules regarding diet and lifestyle, as demonstrated by the wide range of alternatives available today, each the best according to its own ambassadors. However, some ideas from a psychic viewpoint are included here. These are intended to stimulate creative thought and aid the processes described in this book, but they are not definitive rules. As with the visualizations themselves, the only real rule is to use your own judgment.

FASTING

Abstinence is an effective way of preparing yourself for any ritual.

In this era of nutrition-paranoia, instead of being liberated by the ready availability of food, we seem more enslaved by it than ever. We are taught that if we skip breakfast, don't eat three meals a day, or neglect to take our vast selection of food supplement tablets, we will surely fall to bits. Of course, a good balanced diet is helpful, but numerous ascetics have demonstrated that it is not what we eat that keeps us alive, but the life-giving energy, prana, contained by the food. Many individuals, called renunciants, are able, by use of breathing and meditation techniques, to assimilate energy through the medulla oblongata (at the top of the spine, opposite the throat chakra), thus taking their nutrition from the light and air rather than by mouth. They exist quite healthily on as little as a mouthful of rice a day, if indeed they choose to eat at all.

Obviously, living off light is a little advanced for most of us, not to mention extreme. Our psycho-spiritual bodies are designed to necessitate the quest for food. As Giri Bala, one of India's noneating saints, puts it in Paramahansa Yogananda's *Autobiography of a Yogi* (Self-Realization Fellowship, 1990): "It appears that misery, starvation, and disease are whips of our karma that ultimately drive us to seek the true meaning of life."

Conversely, no matter how much food we eat, we will become the living dead if our diet is lacking in spiritual vitamins. The psychic and spiritual state may be improved, however, by following a few time-honored rules: moderation in all things, and the simpler the diet, the better. Boredom, however, should be avoided.

For psychic energy of a healthful nature, moderate fasting can be beneficial. It is common in magick to forego alcohol and tobacco for several days prior to a ritual, along with overindulgent foods and possibly caffeine. The Druids purified their systems and induced visions by eating only apples and drinking only apple juice for three days prior to their ceremonies; of course, they were unable to diversify as we can today.

It is best not to embark upon a fast if you are at work or are required to exert your body during the day. It will harm you more to feel exhausted than it will to break your fast: use your common sense.

Diet and Exercise

Vegetables and fruit are the best pranic energy-givers, particularly if their vivifying qualities are consciously considered and absorbed while chewing.

The color of food is also important, and is a mode of vibrant energy in itself. Red foods—tomatoes, strawberries, radishes, or red apples—are good for strength and determination, and can be consciously used to encourage the red base chakra, which dictates much of our energy-flow.

Green vegetables will certainly contribute toward a healthy heart chakra; green peppers, broccoli, and spinach are among the best. White garlic will have an overall cleansing effect. For general pranic energy, fresh carrots and broccoli are especially good, as are mangoes and the greens mentioned.

Deep-colored foods are excellent, particularly if you wish, as suggested, to visualize the relevant colored chakra being energized as you eat. For the solar plexus chakra, which, if healthy, will keep you emotionally stable and focused on your goal, orange-yellow substances are best: yellow pepper, fresh orange juice, pumpkin, saffron rice, or ghee bread. You could try creating a meal with ingredients for every chakra in turn—though the throat and third eye may prove a challenge when blueberries are out of season (luckily, black currant juice is available all year round). The point, however, is not so much what you eat as your awareness of feeding and maintaining your energy centers. It is keeping the wheels of your body oiled.

It is best to avoid meat and meat products, which are karmic as well as physical pollutants. As W. E. Butler points out in *Magic and the Qabalah*, the elementals that hang around butcher's shops and abattoirs are enough to put the most avid carnivore off meat for life. Only entities that thrive on fear and misery take sustenance from matter saturated in these emotions. Chemical injections and supermarket packaging, especially enhanced by the corporate aura, add to the pernicious qualities of meat.

Grain foods and dairy products can be aura enhancers; cheese is renowned for bringing vivid dreams, and with good reason. There is a strong connection between food and spirituality; the followers of Krishna recognize this and eat only the purest substances (fresh vegetables, fruits, grains, and milk products). Their clean auras generally reflect this. Still, any good food eaten with mental grace, as opposed to mindlessly wolfed, will have a positive effect on one's psychic constitution.

Obviously, an overzealous diet will cause depression and imbalance, especially if your favorite foods are not included, so it is best to cut yourself a little slack. There is no need to feel guilty over a few potato chips or an occasional slice of cheesecake; the etheric body is a good example of "a little of what you like goes a long way." Some metabolisms (whose needs go much deeper than the physical, especially if one is magickally or psychically active) require larger amounts of salt than is commonly recommended, or run well on very spicy foods (chili pepper is a popular stimulant), or enjoy the surplus energy provided by sugar. It is always preferable to listen to your own body rather than to general advice; nobody can be as specifically attuned to your individual requirements as your own Higher Self.

These guidelines apply equally to exercise. You should create a regime that suits your personal biorhythms, rather than disappointing yourself by failing to keep up with somebody else's physical specifications. Some people thrive on a no-holds-barred charge into exercise, and it is true that the burning sensation of muscle rising to the occasion can become addictive: "No pain, no gain" is a popular mantra of this school of thought. The obvious risk is muscle strain and the danger of abandoning the effort because of the ensuing discomfort. For magickal purposes, regular gentle exercise such as walking, aerobics, and swimming will be adequate when combined with meditation and creative visualization. (See Artemis for changing body shape.)

Yogic Relaxation Techniques

Before performing most of the visualizations, it is important to be in a tranquil state of mind. Should the reader find this difficult, the following exercises are recommended. They are likely to relax you almost to the point of sleep, and aid the dream visions included in the visualizations.

Technique 1

Sit cross-legged, or upright in a chair if this more comfortable.

Imagine above you two etheric vats, one vibrant with golden light, the other glowing with an intriguing silver hue. They look like tools of the celestial alchemist, but ineffably pure. The energy they contain seems to be swirling like tiny pulsars around the vats. Some of it is already floating down in your direction.

With these energies in your mind's eye, place your right hand at the center of your forehead and cover your right nostril with the thumb of this hand. Then, with the fourth finger, cover your left nostril.

Remove the thumb from your right nostril, mentally connect with the energy in the golden vat, and breathe in slowly to the count of four. As you do this, see the golden light particles streaming up your right nostril and into your system.

Make your breaths deep, but not so deep that your lungs are bursting; you need to hold the air in for the count of four. Cover both nostrils as you do so.

Once you have held your breath to the count of four, release the left nostril and exhale through it.

Now remove your fingers from both, again to the count of four.

With your hand still at the center of your forehead, replace your thumb over your right nostril, fix your thoughts on the silver vat, and breathe in through the left. As you do so, you notice the silver light ebbing up your left nostril and into your system. Feel the slightly menthol sensation as it touches you and begins to seep like mist into your body.

Covering both nostrils, again hold your breath for four counts.

Maintaining the position of your fourth finger over the left nostril, exhale through the right.

Again, uncover both nostrils to the count of four.

Repeat the process from the beginning.

Continue until you are replete with right-gold and left-silver energies. When you are ready to stop, imagine the two streams of light entwining with one another down your spine, interlacing as they are absorbed.

TECHNIQUE 2

Lie flat on your back, preferably on the floor rather than on a bed, where you may drift off.

With your hands resting palms upward, imagine a cloud of bright golden light enveloping you. As it permeates your body, feel yourself growing happy and relaxed.

All of your muscles are losing their tension: scalp, face, neck, shoulders, chest, arms, hands, stomach, back, legs, feet, and toes. You feel physically liquid, like molten gold. The bright light still darts all around you, revitalizing as it relaxes.

Slowly and deeply, inhale the golden light.

Very slowly, exhale it again.

Wait for as long as you are comfortable before taking the next deep, golden breath.

Repeat the process.

As you inhale and exhale, feel the golden light being taken through your lungs into the bloodstream and carried around your body, causing your skin to glow luminously from the inside. As you breathe, continue to build up your mental image of this ever-growing, ever-glowing aura, until it saturates every atom of your body and extends at least a few feet from your supine body.

When you feel as golden as a sun deity and as relaxed as any divinity-blessed being, you are ready to arise and begin the visualizations.

Index to Goddess Functions

Purpose	Goddess
Abuse, coping with	Kali
Amends, making	Nephthys
Athletics	Artemis
Attraction	
–of a sexual partner	Aphrodite
–of a long-term partner	Isis
–of money	Laksmi
Balance	Iris, Maat
Beauty	Aphrodite, Artemis
Body shape, changing	Artemis, Sekhmet
Chakras, conditioning	Iris
Change	
–accepting	Persephone
–encouraging	Sarasvati
Coming out	Durga
Complacency	
–challenging	Kali
–attaining	Hathor, Laksmi
Communication skills	Iris
Confidence	Durga
Creativity	Sarasvati
Depression, combating	Persephone, Sarasvati
Desire	Aphrodite
Diplomacy	Iris
Discrimination, combating	Hecate, Maat
Divination	Isis
Endurance	Hathor
Exam performance	Sarasvati

Purpose	Goddess
Exorcising the past	Kali, Persephone
Faithfulness	Isis
Fertility	Hathor, Isis
Friendship, creating against the odds	Hecate
Getting even	Durga, Hecate, Kali, Maat
Growth	Hathor
Happiness	Laksmi
Healing	Isis, Nephthys, Sarasvati
Inspiration	Sarasvati
Integration	Hecate, Iris
Intuition	Isis
Justice	Hecate, Maat
Love	
–attaining long term	Isis
–attaining sexual	Aphrodite
–letting go temporarily	Radha
–letting go permanently	Radha
Magickal ability	Isis
Money	Laksmi
Nurturing	Hathor
Phobias, overcoming	Kali
Physical fitness	Artemis
Prejudice, overcoming	Hecate
Psychism	Hecate, Isis
Separation, coping with or causing	Radha
Sexuality	Aphrodite
Shamanism	Sekhmet
Shapeshifting	Sekhmet, Isis

Purpose	Goddess
Strength	
–emotional	Durga, Kali
–physical	Artemis
Study	Sarasvati
Stuck in the mud; escaping	Sarasvati
Success	Laksmi
Truth	Maat
Weight gain/loss	Artemis
Witchcraft skills	Hecate, Isis, Persephone, Sekhmet
Wisdom	Hecate, Maat

HINDU GODDESSES

SARASVATI

Usually she can be found by the sacred river's edge, her black hair flowing in waves down the back of her moon-white sari, the air alive with the mellifluous sound of her vina. Sarasvati's fingers on the tense strings cause golden ages to arise, and when she ceases from her craft, civilizations fall and humanity is diminished.

Sometimes she sits in mantric meditation, a crescent moon upon her forehead, drawing deities from her potent spoken spells. Sometimes she crafts them into yantras, geometric shapes infused with Vedic energy. These she may give as rewards to her favorite wordmongers and winsome minstrels wandering lost in the world of delusion.

She will dip her admirers in the river of despair, blacker even than her pure black hair, or make them dance like dervishes into the mire; then on

3

her paramahansa, her pure white swan of infinite transcendence, she will glide to them, offering gifts.

A searing draft of inspiration to unclog the blocked channel; a suddenly discovered forte to the sensitive whose skills seemed useless; an iron will unto the genius whose mind kept slipping sideways into space. Thus will she hone her devotees once they have been douched in the dark and sacred waters.

White as the kunda flower she comes, a fragrant breath of hope floating above the tumultuous depths of ignorance; her gifts of speech, culture, and religious quest the rafts of our spiritual transiting.

Look! Beyond the river lies a gleaming city of many marvels—Sarasvati's citadel of astral gold, as yet uninhabited. A populace big enough to fill it must first brave the treacherous waters, following the Muse . . . and then the metropolis will be theirs. In the meantime, bards may sing and others dream her promise, elevating thought and art, with every aspiration moving one step closer to the fulfillment of Sarasvati's gifts, and of our own sublime potential.

THE NATURE OF SARASVATI AND HER PRACTICAL APPLICATIONS

In the *Rig Veda*, Sarasvati is featured as a river goddess, and consequently, she has associations with fertility and the purity and life-giving properties of water. Her fertility, however, later came to be regarded as cerebral rather than physical; she is the giver of aspiration, imagination, and creativity.

As a metaphor, crossing a river represents a cleansing transition from old to new (see the VI of Swords in the Tarot); thus her connection with healing properties and processes. She is a baptism-epiphany goddess, and guards over the engendered processes. She manifests at the confluence of the Ganges and Yamuna, once India's most sacred site (now part of Bangladesh), strengthening her connection with initiations and religious experiences of an aquatic nature.

Sarasvati is connected with emotions such as nostalgia, hope, and inspiration—the classic ingredients of any poet. She is the Muse, and music, poetry, and scholarly success are among the gifts of her sphere. Thus she is associated with speech (she is sometimes said to derive from the five tongues of Brahma); particularly with creative sound such as Hindu mantras and spoken spells.

Sarasvati is easily accessed through the potent holy syllable "Om." It is Sarasvati who brings abstract emotion and thought into manifestation, giving them credible form. She is widely worshipped in India as the goddess of culture and learning, her spiritual presence in schools and universities equally vital to that of the books and pens that are venerated in conjunction with her.

Sarasvati represents the essence and meaning of the Vedas; thus all knowledge, sacred and secular, originates from her. Riding her white swan she glides above the murky imperfections of the material (earth) plane, the graceful epitome of purity, intelligence, and transcendence. She is divine eloquence. Sarasvati is the *shakti*, the consort and power of Brahma the creator and, like Durga, she displays a universally maternal aspect. The creation of all the worlds and their inhabitants is accredited to Sarasvati and Brahma during their celestial honeymoon, which, like Laksmi's with Vishnu, lasted many ages.

Few female deities in the Hindu religion escape the role of Mataji, being, of course, benefactors of their "children" or devotees. Even Kali may be broached on these terms, and indeed will respond favorably to the trust her "children" must necessarily invest in her. However, where Kali represents destruction and dissolution, Sarasvati, rarely fierce and ever-dreamy, personifies the creative intelligence. As such, she is represented as dazzlingly white; a luminary in the world of dark ignorance. Because she is instigator of the arts, she is matchless in grace and beauty, an expert in the endless variations of the celestial dance. Her name means "the flowing one," and indeed, her form and movements have a liquid quality.

In Sarasvati's four hands are a lute (or *vina*), a book, a rosary, and a discus (or chakra). The lute draws to our attention the relevance of fine arts to personal development; the book symbolizes the secular sciences; thus, she balances academe with emotional arts. The rosary is illustrative of spiritual sciences: yoga, meditation, and mantras. The discus shows that she is not without defense; a chakra properly thrown is a dreadful weapon. It also incorporates into Sarasvati's repertoire of human excellence the dimension of physicality and athletics. She is a balanced goddess, quick to indicate the proper use of our skills to further human development. She is the civilizer, the impulse to evolve, taking us step-by-step from cave painting to computer art. She would rebuke, however, any insular extreme: expressiveness is paramount in her criteria, and all that indicates profound thought and emotion lies in her domain.

Like Krishna, Sarasvati is a favorite with the peacocks; sometimes she even rides on their backs. The thousand eyes of their feathers represent the all-seeing divine nature, while their ostentatious traits are symbolic of the material world. Peacocks are often associated with pride and ignorance, and their alluring beauty can warn of the insidious evils of materialism. However, Sarasvati, being divine, holds the negative aspects of the resplendent bird well in check.

APPROACHING SARASVATI: PREPARATION

Sarasvati presides over evening prayer, so the early evening is an appropriate time to approach her, and the fuller the moon the better, as Sarasvati is said to "shine like many moons" herself. She is sometimes described as being smeared in sandalwood paste, so sandalwood incense is beneficial in evoking her.

Meditation on "Om" prior to these exercises will help immensely. According to *shabda-brahman* (ultimate reality in the form of sound), this syllable embodies the entire creative process, which Sarasvati mediates.

It is preferable to actually make the "Om" sound; vibrate it in your throat and run it up and down your spine and through your chakras— but this depends on your circumstances. Such practices are infinitely valuable, but only if you are uninhibited and not worried that the neighbors will hear you. Practicing in semiprivate areas can be deeply disturbing; footsteps and comments outside the door do little to aid inner tranquillity.

A good alternative to chanting out loud is to purchase one of the several excellent recordings of Tibetan monks that are now becoming widely available. Those of the Tibet Foundation (Bloomsbury Way, off New Oxford Street, London, WC1) are recommended. The atmospherics can be absorbed privately on a personal stereo or by using headphones. These rather alarming-sounding ceremonies contain a high dosage of "Om" and are excellent for helping evoke the sound in one's head. No need to listen to the whole thing prior to the visualization; a sample of a minute or two should suffice.

Sarasvati's *puja* is celebrated in early spring, so buds and spring flowers will also help to create the environment conducive to this goddess.

A lotus or ylang-ylang (an oil that is extracted from the flowers of a ylang-ylang tree) bath will help you relax and get you on the right wavelength.

Look at yourself in a mirror by candlelight and comb your hair while contemplating the perfection and unsullied beauty you are about to encounter; listen to some relaxing music as you prepare (preferably classical). Appreciate the skill, both spiritual and practical, that went into its composition. One would be nothing without the other (we all know of music that is emotional drivel, or conversely, empty melodic structures); this balance is one of Sarasvati's major facets. In her, the practical is elevated by higher feeling, and high-flying ideals are earthed through skill and craftsmanship. She is the force that brings the strands of interlacing harmony to the mind of the musician, who listens and writes, or plays them spontaneously. She is the music of the spheres, an audible sacred geometry. Consider how poetry, sculpture, and innovative art spring up whenever she is near.

When you have relaxed, surrounded yourself with pleasant scents, and performed your candlelit (or twilight) toilette, recontemplate the "Om" sound for a minute or two, or the length of time that feels right to you. You are now ready to encounter Sarasvati on the inner planes.

VISUALIZATION FOR CREATIVE INSPIRATION

Sit cross-legged on your floor or bed. If you can comfortably manage lotus posture, all the better.

Having laid the mantric foundation with the "Om" sound, you are ready to progress to recital of the best mantra for balanced creative pursuits, that of "Om Kring Kring Kring." Strictly speaking, this should be chanted (or muttered while mentally chanting) 1,008 times, and counted out on a rosary. Completing the mantra will guarantee your success, so it is well worth setting aside the time to see it through. It will also create a mood conducive to the following visualization.

The visualization will work on its own, as will the mantra. Choose whichever you prefer, or try them both. Do not be too solemn. Fun is a powerful component in this day and age, and the energy of enjoyment will enhance any spell, meditation, or visualization.

Start this exercise by imagining your base chakra growing dense with energy. Feel the weight of the psychic tension gathering there, and the dull red glow of the unreleased potential.

Gradually, the chakra begins to whir, faster and faster, and as the speed increases, so does the red light flowing from it; at first slowly, then brighter and more effusively. Continue this process until the light-producing motion is firmly established in your mind's eye, and preferably, until you can feel it physically.

Now, mentally link the pulsating, growing energy of your tailbone area with the zone above and between your eyes.

Breathe in deeply and out deeply, aware of the base chakra's light beginning to seep upward as you do so.

Next, deliberately and firmly pull this red energy up your spine toward your third eye area. Notice how the two types of chakra-energy combine to form a deep reddish-indigo.

Your base chakra continues to spin brightly, infused with the purple color from your third eye zone. Now your base chakra, spine, and pineal gland are all glowing with a vibrant indigo-red.

Holding this color strongly in your mind's eye, take a deep breath of light and imagine you are travelling in lotus posture over a vast purple sea whose waves shimmer in a thousand hues of purple and red, creating sharp and subtle colors you have never imagined before.

The sky in which you are levitating is also purple, but a deeper, more intense shade punctuated from time to time by passing distant moons—silvery white orbs whose light seems to make you travel faster and higher. You can change speed and direction with a flick of the switch of will, but at the moment you are happy to be travelling through such a beautiful astral space on your way to supplicate Sarasvati.

After a while you begin to perceive thin silver cords around you, invisible to your outer vision but you can feel them growing thicker; they remind you of the strings of a lute. They seem, on closer inspection, to be vibrating with infinitely pure atoms of carefully plucked sound. There are many of them being sounded at once, and you are travelling faster still into the heart of this symphony, your vision sharp and senses rejoicing in this astral wonder.

Now, call to Sarasvati.

Ask her to allow you to approach her in search of inspiration.

All around you are tiny atoms of pranic energy, vibrating very quickly and making you envision each as a universe in its own right. Your body is also charged with positive energy: the prana is permeating you even as you hang in Sarasvati's sacred space.

Before you know it, a glowing white figure sitting serenely on a swan is gliding toward you. You can see the tiny red light of her bindi from here, like a drop of blood on snow. Gracefully you begin to fly toward her, still in lotus posture. Even as you think it you arrive, touching her feet in humility.

Sarasvati's hand alights on your crown chakra, sending vivid shots of energy into your brain and down your spinal chord. The purple sky, which you know is saturated with all the energy of all the universes, is being absorbed into your body via the top of your head, your ears, your mouth, and your neck.

Look at Sarasvati and, when you feel fully charged with creative ability and potential, thank her.

Wait for Sarasvati to depart before you do. Be sure not to turn your back on her—social graces are important to this goddess. Politeness will be rewarded, but rudeness and laziness are anathema to Sarasvati, most courteous of goddesses.

Observe everything you experience as she leaves and as you return, and when you do, open your eyes, have a stretch, and immortalize the experience however you please—write it, paint it, turn it into music. This is the thank-you offering that Sarasvati would most desire.

VISUALIZATION FOR SELF-HEALING: AIDING TRANSITION AND CHANGE

Sarasvati can also be approached for healing powers, for yourself and others, especially if the ailment is psychological and connected with trauma or maladjustment to change. Depression after a bereavement, or agoraphobia as a result of an unwelcome move or loss of social status are examples of Sarasvati's potential healing domain. She helps us transcend our concerns and take a fatalistic overview—in its most positive sense. A true Hindu neither celebrates good nor bemoans loss, and is aware that circumstances on this plane are continually in flux and their pleasures and pains are merely transitory; in some respects Sarasvati embodies this belief. However, the intense experiences are not simply endured, but are sublimated into the arts; thus, even the destructive becomes creative.

A visualization along this vein could bring you the necessary zest and courage to break out of a low period and try something creative and new; anything from making yourself an unusual meal to writing a novel. Sarasvati teaches us that everything happens for a positive purpose, and she can help us cross that difficult river of change, be cleansed, and reach the shore in safety.

Sit quietly, shut your eyes, and mentally gather together all of your negative feelings about the situation you have been undergoing. Think of the things you would like to leave behind—those aspects of your life that have been hindering your progression. Bundle all of your hurt, disappointment, and reticence into a big black bag; take as long as you need to strongly feel and envision this process.

Now, visualize yourself standing at a river's edge. This side of the bank represents your past, the river is the process of change, and on the other side awaits your new liberated life.

Take the black bag of woes and bury it by the water's edge. Again, take as long as you need to properly complete this task.

Feeling relieved, if a little rootless, you resolve to cross the river to inhabit your new life. In you wade, until you are waist-deep in water. Behind you is everything that has become obsolete in your life, and all of the negative feelings about the situation you have been enduring. Notice how the ground feels beneath your feet: rocky, slippery, sandy. The water itself represents your present state of being, and it may be murky, clear, fast-moving, tranquil, or turmoiled; your inner eye will tell you how it is. Either way, you know that the stretch of river before you is very deep and that you are likely to have difficulty sustaining your direction. You are doubtful as to whether you can make it to the other side.

For a moment or two, contemplate how you are going to cross. Think of all the good things waiting for you on the other side—your creature comforts, company, exciting new experiences. Try to feel enthusiasm for this future, even if only because it has to be better than your present situation. You will need to employ all of your will power to help you across. Determine not to be washed downstream or deflected from your course.

You cast your inner eye around for something to help you reach the opposite bank. It looks quite inviting now, but there is a danger of being swept away if you forge any farther ahead.

Suddenly, you see a swan of brilliant white floating down the river toward you. On its back is a woman in white robes, resplendent and smiling. Your main impression of her is a mass of flowing white light, intelligent and angelic. As she glides toward you, try to mentally connect with her and ask for her help.

Explain to Sarasvati why you are stuck; describe the problem that initiated your depression or stultification, and emphasize that you are eager to reach the other side of the river and the new life that waits for you there. Take as long as you need for this prayer-like supplication.

When you emerge from your inner monologue, you find that a large lotus leaf is floating beside the swan.

With a swish of her slender hand Sarasvati invites you to climb onto the leaf. She tells you to concentrate on reaching the other side of the river, and as you focus, you start to move.

You are aware that Sarasvati is behind you, ready to help if any trouble occurs.

As you draw closer to the river bank you notice a small temple with the "Om" sign painted on it, red against yellow. There is wonderful, strange music coming out of the temple, and its unusual architecture fascinates you. Its stained glass windows are amazingly crafted, and intense inspiring colors beam from the building.

When you reach the other side of the river, dismount and step with assurance onto the new terrain. You turn to thank the goddess, but she is gone.

Excited by the adventure and eager to explore this new land so full of beautiful intriguing things, you head for the temple in order to thank Sarasvati.

No sooner have you thought it than your feet rise off the ground and you are delivered to the threshold, where a potent wave of billowing incense and vibrant sound engulfs you.

Feel the "Om" running up and down your spine, through your limbs, jiggling every atom of your body. In the smoky sound flash all kinds of colors; subtle and vivid shades, pulsating violet hues, and streaks of red and flowing blue.

If you are wearing shoes at this point, kick them off before you cross the temple threshold.

As you enter, you feel as if your body is being shaken by incredible mechanical thunder, but you welcome it as you know it is breaking up the clay straight-jacket of your previous monotonous existence, and exposing the brighter subtle body beneath it.

Soon, you are feeling very light and agile and are impatient to explore this new land in your new vehicle.

Find the shrine and pluck a candle, a string of flowers, or a cake from the ether; place it at the foot of the altar, and thank Sarasvati for guiding you into the next cycle of your incarnation.

Now, leave the temple and come back to your body; remember that you are anxious to get out and experience all the wonderful things this new land has to offer. You will deliberately seek the unusual.

Open your eyes and, when you are ready, write down everything you have experienced in this visualization. Analyze it if you so desire (what or who did you see when you were looking for help to reach the other side? Does the water seem calmer to you now, in retrospect? What were you standing on before you were rescued?). Perhaps you will even start a dream-diary now—why not? The imagination is a fascinating thing, after all, and who's to say that one reality is any more substantial than another?

ACADEMIC EXCELLENCE: PREPARATION

Sarasvati is the ideal deity to whom to appeal in the cause of academe. By appealing to her you will please her; Sarasvati loathes sterile learning, but logical effort combined with passion and inspiration will gain her favor. The practical and the spiritual must combine. This is a cause particularly fitting to India herself, a country whose spirituality far outweighs its utilitarianism. This imbalance was underlined at the time of the Raj, when India was invaded by those of the opposite make-up. As Jodh Singh points out in *The Wild Sweet Witch* (Philip Mason, Penguin 1947/88), "It is true that we are impractical, visionaries, dreamers . . . it is because we put the spirit first and these Europeans always think of the material. This is why they are our masters, but the things of the spirit are more important, and there they are children." In Sarasvati, if not in her native country, we find the balance between these extremes; a combination of the best features of each element.

The following meditation is simple and best performed in the morning before you begin to make changes or work, or on the day of examination.

Lavender oil may be evaporated in the room or used in the bath prior to this exercise. This is a good mental tonic and handy when concentration is required.

VISUALIZATION FOR ACADEMIC EXCELLENCE

Sitting cross-legged on the floor or bed, imagine yourself inside a giant purple egg. This egg is Akasha, the symbol of all knowledge and the pool of all revelation.

Chant or whisper the mantra "Om Aim Kling Saum Saraswatiye Namaha" as many times as you feel inclined. Feel the sharpness of your intellect as you sit there, your keen desire to learn, and the spiritual presence of Sarasvati, who presides over all educational matters.

Admire the deep unusual purple that fills the air around you; in it abides every atom of creative intelligence from the source of the ancient cave-paintings to the inspiration of Mozart. This is the origin of every theory on life, death, and the universe; every terrestrial and spiritual achievement.

Nearby, shelves heave with the weight of many books.

A faint smell of incense hangs in the air; a hint of an arcane ritual that makes you contemplate the esoteric contents of the tomes. Underlying this is the scent of the books themselves; the pervasive library smell of aging pages.

Feel yourself being elevated by visiting this sacred space.

Now, breathe in deeply and concentrate on your crown and pineal chakras; connect yourself with this incredible pool of illumination. When you breathe out, imagine the channels of your perception being cleared, creating an information superhighway of your mind.

Continue to breathe consciously in and out until the relationship between you and the Akashic information is firmly established and unquestionable.

Now, imagine your aura fired in purple, like a flame. You are becoming a luminary.

Your resolve is strengthened; you know your capacity to be infinite. You can absorb wisdom and inspiration through your crown chakra and third eye at will; your potential is limitless.

Return to the room braced and alert, and apply yourself methodically to your study or the matter in hand. This, combined with your awareness of higher things and a clever originality, cannot fail to aid you in the realms of creative academe.

MUNDANE ARCHETYPES

The Sarasvati character displays dreamy tendencies in youth, and her academic achievements, though showing signs of promise, are not outstanding until later in life. She displays an early penchant for music, dance, and poetry, preferring these more evocative arts to dry academe.

If she is denied creative expression or imaginative stimulation she will become sullen or sorrowful. Spiritual matters and imagery inspire her: she may join the local Christian group. Facts and figures mean nothing to her until she can attach them to some aspect of her emotional life, which she will begin to do in her teenage years, at which time she is also likely to grow out of her initial religious proclivities and into something more independent and meaningful. Her emotional life will become intense, inspired, and full of dark nights of the soul followed by radiant epiphanies.

The Sarasvati-type will pick her partners from the realms of culture: art galleries, poetry readings, opera houses, and university staff rooms are likely cruising venues. She has a strong desire to nurture and learn from her partner, and in youth will inevitably raise the latter to new creative heights before she is abandoned for another, more sophisticated Muse.

In early life she seems sweet and idealistic; later, her sharp intelligence evolves in accordance with her personal development and, after many ups and downs, she discovers her academic ability and may well become a formidable bluestocking, whose work is kept from dryness by the constant irrigation of emotional intelligence.

The life of the Sarasvati archetype is usually characterized by harmonious relationships with friends and family. She will discover her innate eloquence as her confidence increases; for example, with age. She is the type of woman whose life begins at forty.

Tarot Cards
The Queen of Cups, IV Wands, VI Swords, VIII Cups.

Durga

Durga the demon-slayer fights clad in her glad rags, her elegance hypnotic and her frailty beguiling.

Mountains of purple rise up behind her, capped by sacred snows and haunted by yogis whose thoughts reach her easily in this pristine atmosphere.

Pockets of ethereal perfume float from the folds of her sari, enticing the senses of the next eager lover. Delicately, she slays.

As ripe and mellow as a harvest moon she seems, her ten arms poised as if to cut and gather her own crop of bright blessings and hand it to her opponent in surrender; a cunning trick!

Suitors wait in line to challenge her in battle; what better salve to the injured male pride than the taming of this celestial shrew? A million men have lent their virility to Durga, gem of femininity; their admiration only makes her independence stronger.

See how she digs those elegant fingers into her war-steed's soft neck fur. At her bidding, subtle as a snake's, he carries Durga to some favored vantage point, watched by the envious eyes of her opponents. The beast's luxuriant purrings torment them with longing, but his mistress' martial arts keep them ever at bay.

Rather death in the propeller-blades of her arms than this humiliating demise-by-desire.

So they come, one by one, to be unmanned by the skillful swoop of a tender blade-taloned hand, and behind the mirage that is Durga, behold the victorious smile of her kindred spirit, Kali.

With their dying breath they must admit that they misjudged her strength, her nature, and her source.

Durga throws back her beautiful head and laughs. At the sound of her ambrosial merriment, a hundred more step forward for the challenge.

Thus she appears to the enemies of peace, and thus they are conquered.

Durga is pacifying and beautiful, but a formidable enemy. She was originally created from rays of concentrated thought when the male gods could do nothing to combat a particularly fierce demon. The rays—crimson, white, and lustrous black—danced together in the air, merging and forming a pillar of blinding radiance. From this stepped a being of unsurpassed beauty sitting on a lion.

Joyfully, the gods lent Devi, as she was then known, the sum of their strength and full use of their celestial weapons, and sent her fresh into mortal combat with the world-threatening demon Durga. After a gory victory, Devi adopted the name Durga, indicative of her frightful powers. Next she faced the formidable buffalo-demon Mahisha. Once again the delusion of frailty won her the battle, along with her martial ability and tactical skill.

When angry, she is closely associated with Kali; indeed, Kali is sometimes produced as an embodiment of Durga's fury, and they have fought side by side against many demons—always, of course, emerging victorious.

The most important aspect of Durga in the context of this book is her independence. She uses her "male" power to fulfill her own ends, and she is never personally compromised. One translation of her name is "Unapproachable One," referring to her physical location—normally, isolated mountainous regions; it also refers to her refusal to interact personally with her suitors or supplicants, unless, of course, she is slaying them.

Being the personification of all the power of good in the cosmos, Durga is overwhelming and difficult to define, exacerbating her quality of distance, particularly from the male or demonic of the species. However, she may be approached on a more personal level as mother of the universe, *Mataji*, in her kindly and pleasant aspect, or, for women, as an exemplar of inner strength and overriding intelligence.

Durga's requirement from a suitor is that he must be able to defeat her in battle. Naturally this is impossible and, though entire armies rise to the challenge, Durga remains unfettered by a husband. Her role as sustainer of cosmic balance ensures that her opponents are primarily demons whose excessive vanity leads them to believe in Durga's vulnerability to their attack. In some scriptures she is coupled with Siva, but it is in her maiden aspect that she evinces the most power and is therefore at optimum capacity to help us as supplicants.

Durga is a powerful ally in challenging social stereotypes. She may be broached, for example, for the strength required to be single, which is still, in this liberated age, considered a little weird; or in matters challenging the ideals of marriage or monogamy; or for the strength required to come out of the closet and sustain a relationship with a same-sex partner. Anything that flies in the face of convention, particularly male-imposed convention, is appropriate to Durga.

Females are no longer perceived only in relation to their men—as daughters, wives, and mothers. Durga is a good role model for women, Hindu or otherwise, who wish to burn brightly in their own right; particularly those who refuse to compromise the positive points of their femininity in their cause. She symbolizes women who employ every aspect of themselves to get what they want; in some respects, she is the antithesis of Radha.

Durga is a rebel; like Kali, she eats and drinks metaphorical meat and wine (taboo substances to the Hindu), which she is free to do because of her cosmic composition, fashioned from a will to see justice done. Durga provides us with a little indulgence, a little leeway in the cause of a higher good. She refutes parochial ideals and substitutes them with an elegant alternative, always highly original. Durga safeguards the integral individuality of women.

She stands on a tiger or a lion, appropriately the Tarot symbol for strength (see the *Tarot of the Old Path* for an apt illustration of the freedom Durga can bestow), and in a cosmic context she is said to simultaneously create, maintain, and destroy the world, confirming her to be an amalgam of all deities. She is also the power of sleep, being in control of reality-levels, and may be approached for aid in matters pertaining to this and astral travel.

Carrying an array of weapons that are not for decorative purposes only, Durga has Kali's abilities without her wanton ferocity. This baffling goddess, with her beauty and her physical power, her modes of action and suspension of activity, her ability to destroy or to heal, may be summarized as an embodiment of strength. It is for this quality then, in any of its variants, that we shall approach her.

Approaching Durga: Preparation

Autumn is the best time to approach Durga, but of course we cannot always pick our season, so try to work with a full moon on the brink of waning, or use yellow, brown, and orange candles and a pinch of sandalwood and frankincense on a charcoal disk or in stick form—whatever feels autumnal to you.

If you are a Leo, try to tap into your leonine nature; its arrogance can be of use when "defying convention," though be sure to balance it with a healthy heart-chakra: you do not want to trample roughshod over the feelings of others. Durga is not, like Kali, implacable once stirred; she sympathizes with other's points of view, but does her own thing anyway because she believes it to be right. She takes power from the male gods and deceives others with her feminine appearance—then slays them— but only to preserve *dharma*, or universal balance. She is a confrontational version of Maat.

Thus Durga is the ideal goddess to approach when we have a strong sense of overriding justification about something that challenges others' less-considered standards. Her lightning bolt, thunderbolt, trident, and discus are formidable weapons designed to further the cause of good in the Universe; personal rectitude is essential. It is helpful to meditate a while on your cause and fill yourself with indignation before you visualize Durga. Tapping into her character traits will, as with any deity, help you to channel her.

Visualization for Strength

Once you have created a suitably fiery autumnal atmosphere and a rightful sense of indignation, take a couple of deep golden breaths and begin to visualize this incredibly beautiful, strong, and feminine goddess mounted on her lion, her ten arms fanning around her shoulders with supernatural potential and ability.

The tools Durga carries range from a dagger to a discus to a conch shell; in each deceptively slender white hand she holds a peacekeeping weapon. She has complete mastery of the beast she rides, indicating her absolute transcendence of baser instincts such as greed and lust.

As Durga's image becomes clearer in your mind, a strong feeling of quiet respect flows from you to the goddess. You admire her discipline and ability. Mentally bow at her gold-sandaled feet, giving obeisance to the deity whose skills you wish to emulate.

Now, ask Durga for her help. Notice that even the skin of her feet emanates a surreal golden glow; as you look up you see that her robes are as red as blood and richly ornamented with precious glinting gems and burnished metals.

Look into her eyes. They are dark and bewitching, infinitely beguiling; their softness is counteracted only by the green of the third eye above and between them. This eye carries a different message; one of unrelenting determination and sublime detachment. Durga is a beautiful witch, a Kali when stirred. Nothing can deter her, for she knows she will always win—she has proved it to herself time and time again. She would not be here were this not the case.

Admire the goddess for a while, then imagine that you are becoming her. Smell the slightly ferrous scent of her robes, the sandalwood aroma of her skin. Feel your own increased ability as your arms replicate, each new limb symbolic of a past experience and the knowledge conferred by it. Breathe in more of the golden light that fills the air in the vicinity of the deity; feel it heightening your resolve and strengthening your capability.

Now, concentrate hard on your objective.

Think of your achievements in the past—the harder won, the better—and with the help of Durga, determine to add this to the list.

The tingling sensation above your pineal gland is your third eye beginning to glow green.

Continue to inhale the goddess' aura in long deep breaths, aware of this new psychically active zone on your forehead.

Think again of your objective. With your justified anger you will slay the demons that intend to block your path and transform them to subservient inoffensives.

With Durga as your guide, tackle your obstacles mentally. Durga is within you; you need make reference to nobody else. You are utterly strong and entirely independent, requiring nobody's aid; you are a goddess in your own right.

Determine, like Durga, to drive the chariot of your own fate—feel your own aura begin to glow yellow and then red with determination, strength, and hope. Keep breathing in these emotions and colors; pack them into your psychic battery for future use. Charge yourself with surprise reserves of strength.

Now, when your tirelessly sanguine persona is fully established and your will is as hard as iron, make moves to confront your obstacles. Do not forget to employ your considerable charms in your cause. The sooner you can approach the situation of enmity, the better.

Make sure you look and feel good, and hold the image of yourself as Durga in your mind. Use to optimum capacity the beauty you know you possess, inner and outer.

Keep your aura golden; if the situation turns nasty, switch it to red, but maintain your composure.

Mentally project the image of yourself as Durga at the other person's third eye area. Do not allow their words or actions, however harsh, to ruffle your image of your strong, independent Durga-self.

State your case or do your thing, as appropriate. Chances are they will not be able to resist. But even if they do, you know you'll win—Durga always does.

MUNDANE ARCHETYPES

The Durga archetype is a freedom-fighter, a champion of just causes. She is socially adept and well-respected within her own peer group, using her good background to further her unconventional projects. She avoids sanctimony by being proactive in her approach, and by practicing what she preaches to an uncompromising degree.

Despite the importance of her background as a foundation and source of support, the Durga woman is not afraid to fly in the face of firmly set standards or to act independently, particularly when her ire is up. She may, conversely, seek to please authority figures and the generations above herself; she has an inveterate sense of hierarchy.

She is feared by her enemies for her unrelenting tenacity and absolute self-belief. She can be belligerent, arrogant, and venomous, and needless to say, is a menace when misguided. As a career woman she will rise quickly and ruthlessly to the top, where she will be both admired and despised.

On the other side of the coin she is rarely happier than in the comfort of her own home, which she would readily share with the children and animals—especially dogs—of which she is (sometimes secretly) so fond.

She may not marry a man; if she does, he will have to be of impressive psycho-spiritual stature, and successful in his own right. The Durga-woman does not tolerate weakness in the opposite sex, though she is likely to be more lenient with her own. The lesbian Durga-type admires feminine women and falls for those she feels she can protect. However, her enthusiasm for gender politics may lead her to compromise her traditionally "feminine" traits, giving her the semblance of being masculine. She will deliberately provoke this perception in other people, and may view men as the enemy.

Heterosexual and chic lesbian Durgas are likely to maintain a slick femininity which, coupled with an aura of power, gives rise to much admiration. However, many of her archetypal expressions will remain celibate or are serially monogamous.

No matter what the proclivity of the Durga-woman, she is always the subject and object of strong passions.

Tarot Cards
Strength, Queen of Swords.

KALI

In a temple in Dakshineswar a young yogi is praying devoutly before a stone image of Kali. For many hours he has meditated on the scorching stone floor, awaiting her animation in his inner vision, a sure sign of her audience.

Eventually, she rewards his faith. Her third eye clicks open, glaring down on him, veined by blood. She smiles, her lips a noose about his astral body; her fangs yawning, yellow, putrid.

One by one her limbs begin to move; a dark and potent light flows from her head, her four arms, her fulsome body. Stepping down from her lofty altar she slinks toward the prostrate devotee, her necklace of human heads swinging to and fro, her skirt of severed arms arresting all possibility of kinetic action. Kali's hand hovers about the yogi's smiling head and touches it on the crown. A lightening bolt of spiritual enlightenment shatters his former illusions. The yogi's boon is granted.

THE NATURE OF KALI AND HER PRACTICAL APPLICATIONS

Kali is the apotheosis of Nature. She is, therefore, the embodiment of duality: with two hands she gives; with two she destroys. She is as frightening as she is inevitable; like death, disease, demise, none can escape her. In India, where conditions are harsh and unpredictable, it is not surprising that a goddess of such violent temperament has been conceived.

Kali guards against complacency; who would fail to take precautions with such a fierce, demanding goddess breathing down one's neck? Pride and materialism become impossible when Kali is present.

To the yogi, Kali is God made manifest in Mother Nature; and the mystic knows God to be eternally graceful. Her name, indeed, derives from *Kali Ma*, meaning *black mother*, not necessarily a contradiction in terms. To a being already attuned to immortality, Kali in all her gore represents the fleeting and liberating experience of being reborn into spirit, and consequently, is not to be feared, but to be welcomed. His subjective reality of Kali as beneficent is made manifest in her enlightening aspect. She may look terrifying, but the yogi understands this to be a blessing. Consequently, the great goddess blesses him.

The message underlying Kali's iconography is that we are not merely flesh and that creation is not merely material. It is for this reason that those following a spiritual path in India are encouraged to meditate at night, in a graveyard, naked, and with dishevelled hair, chanting Kali's mantra. There is something of the principle of *familiarity breeds contempt* in this; the scariest Halloween is lived through and nothing happens. That is to say, demons run riot in the mind, specters terrorize the soul, but one is still alive in the morning to tell the tale.

The cremation-ground and battlefields are Kali's domain; she is normally depicted surrounded by dead and dying bodies. The severed head and bloodied sword she holds exhibit her role as supreme energy responsible for the dissolution of the universe. Another hand is raised in blessing.

Kali, like her consort Siva, goes sky-clad, or naked; she is, quite literally, divinity unveiled. Her wild hair represents her limitless freedom. In Hinduism, creative sound is the source of all manifestations (hence the great significance of mantras); by wearing a necklace of fifty human heads, representative of the fifty letters of the Sanskrit alphabet, Kali symbolically suspends the creative capacity.

The profound black of her skin and of the tantric blood-pit are those of the void in which intellectual concepts cease to have any meaning. Likewise, her skirt of arms indicates the cessation of physical activity. In Kali, our lives are suspended between worlds. She represents death, and the period between incarnations when the shock of death still lingers. She is the reigning goddess of traumatic transitions.

As well as epitomizing the qualities of blackness, the name Kali derives from *Kala*, one meaning of which is "time." As such, she represents the origin of limited power; through her each life is cauterized, made finite. She is often depicted with one foot planted on Siva's prostrate body; the position by which he halted one of her particularly grisly death-dances. On one hand this indicates the power of higher emotions within Kali's psyche, even at its most negative; on the other it shows her as the dynamic shakti-energy of Siva or Brahman, without which they would be beyond thought and action, and too lofty for the world of mortals. Kali's root is in eternity, but she defines our material reality. What Siva dreams, Kali realizes and sets into motion. Thus we see that all energies, all godforms, act in reference to other energies and godforms. Nothing is separate.

As an embodiment of the wrath of more benign goddesses, Parvati for example, Kali represents justified anger. She is brought into being to destroy demons; usually, beings who have performed formidable penances, gained boons of the gods, and then abused their power. She often intercedes on behalf of the less powerful. She is sometimes said to spring from Durga's forehead, the goddess epitomizing benevolence at its most bellicose. In conjunction with Kali and Durga's righteous fury spring up the *Matrikas*, or "little mothers," their seven fearsome helpers.

In a similar manner to Sekhmet, Kali is intoxicated by bloodlust. When she fights the self-replicating demon Raktavija, it is her ability to drunkenly imbibe that makes her victorious. Prior to her arrival on the battlefield, Kali's rival has been able to produce a thousand warriors from a single drop of blood. With such an army the demon is insurmountable, a threat to divine order and certainly to mankind. Incensed by his arrogance, mild Parvati manifests as all-consuming Kali and sups every drop of Raktavija's blood before it has the power to reproduce. Her wrath is entirely immune to niceties. When roused, Kali is terrible indeed.

In India, where female infanticide, high maternal mortality, domestic violence, and the neglect of women's health means there are 10 percent fewer women than there should be, justified anger as expressed by a female deity is more than a little appropriate. According to the Indian National Crime Bureau, every twenty-six minutes one woman is molested, every forty-three minutes one woman is kidnapped to be sold to a brothel, and every fifty-four minutes one is raped. It is barely surprising that Kali is a popular symbol for the worldwide women's movement. As Divine Nature, she refutes all that is unnatural to the soul. Thus, she is a suitable goddess to whom to appeal to help terminate cycles of abuse.

Kali reveals the presence of chaos and rebellion; she may choose to elevate or to destroy—her decision must be trusted. As Nature, there is no going against her. The best we can do is to relax and enjoy the ride. Thus the devotee sitting in the dark graveyard undergoes fear, fights it, dissolves into it, and eventually transcends it. He emerges in the morning (hopefully) devoid of fear of death. He realizes that he is already dead, and that the so-called dead are already living. Kali-Kala-Time is an illusion. All is now. We have to trust; like many areas of Hinduism, the Kali philosophy encourages a certain liberating fatalism. Kali says "face the fear and do it anyway." She encourages her devotees to combat their ghouls by bringing them into the light of conscious recognition. In giving reference to the fear, she challenges complacency; by exhibiting destruction as a part of cosmic order, she helps us overcome the fear itself. There is much benefit to be gained from this apparently monstrous divinity.

Needless to say, child sacrifice may be taking the principle a little too far. The sanitized version of Kali popular in the West, however, is inaccurate. Kali is a bloody goddess whose tongue does not loll for nothing; her major function is to scare us into remembrance of our divine nature. She is anti-ego; that is, against the preciousness of ego. Approaching her is always a risk, and she will respond with a challenge.

While contemplating Kali you will most likely find that issues pertaining to any abuse you may have suffered, particularly sexual abuse, will come to the fore. Fears and phobias are other probable themes. Other goddesses are plain sailing compared to this crazy lady.

Kali causes one to fight; having experienced her, one's personal strength is indubitable because the challenge has been forced and victory, even if psychological and not physical, has been won. She can aid the termination of cycles of abuse by substituting victim-mentality with that of self-preservation, and by transforming what seems to be negative into a radiant strength. With Kali, to have visited the battlefields of the cosmic forces and to have paid personal witness to the struggle between light and darkness is a positive virtue. One cannot fight the darkside until one really knows its essence; the experience, though terrorizing at the time, is ultimately an act of empowerment.

Overcoming Cycles of Abuse

The way we react to abusive situations can define our lives. Some employ past abuse as an excuse for all personal failings; others gain incredible strength when they emerge sane and spiritually whole. Obviously, this may take time; a negative initial response is inevitable and healthy.

There is a balance between being too precious about oneself—"I'd rather die or kill than have anyone so much as touch me without my consent," and the sort of low self-esteem one encounters in sufferers of habitual domestic violence—"I deserve it; I was asking for it really." There is also the issue of admitting, either consciously or out loud, that one is being abused. Situations can be deceptive.

Clare, for example, is in the most glossy of relationships. She and her husband are both successful, well liked, and respected—seemingly a model example of a partnership at its best. This is, of course, an image Clare goes out of her way to perpetuate, perhaps subconsciously, hoping that this external endorsement will somehow filter into the actual relationship and "come true." The fact that she is entirely unfulfilled—she is a legal secretary but has always wanted to travel the world and paint—and is held in place by her husband's ingenious network of guilt trips, is something she can barely bring herself to admit.

Clare's personal freedom has been seriously curtailed. When she so much as phones a friend her husband becomes suspicious, and he frequently accuses her, quite wrongly, of having an affair. Most of his demeaning techniques are much more subtle. Her own weakness has, of course, allowed the situation to perpetuate; but if she begins to break out of the mold she has cast for her life, the very least she can expect is physical and emotional upheaval. In fear of ruining her much-coveted image, and because of general insecurity, she buries her responses in a deep pit of unspoken resentment, and her husband's bad behavior continues unchecked.

Elise, by all appearances an easy-going, intelligent woman, has been in a relationship with Pat, mother of three, for nearly five years. Pat vaunts feminism as the necessary antithesis to men, yet treats Elise with scant respect. She uses her as live-in carer for the children, which Elise does willingly, but the task-sharing is minimal; she is unfaithful and sometimes violent, and goes to incredible lengths to divorce Elise from any friendships that might threaten the relationship; for example, those in which her position as Pat's captive is questioned. The few friends who remain must tailor their opinions to suit Pat, and be syco-phantic for fear of being ousted from Elise's life.

Elise, by self-confession a martyr and nonconfrontationalist, refuses to outwardly acknowledge her partner's emotional abuse and lives in a delusion of feminist ideals. There is, of course, a great deal of pressure on her to prove to the outside world that a lesbian relationship involving children can be functional. In catering to this cause, Elise is bypassing her own needs. It is not, needless to say, their gender or sexuality that causes the problems, but their psychological constitutions.

Elise feels that if the relationship fails, she will be endorsing the prej-udice of her "opponents." Because she has, to some extent, defined her personality by these ideals, it would take a great deal more self-confi-dence than Pat allows her to harbor to break out of the situation. She also cares deeply for Pat's children, and is reluctant to disrupt their lives. Like Clare, she is too scared to take that plunge of consciousness; and when-ever she does, she convinces herself she is being selfish. Pat does all she can to perpetuate this standpoint before storming out and leaving Elise with the kids.

Elise's essential cause is indubitably a worthy one, but in supporting it in this manner she has become the antithesis of an empowered woman, accepting orders and creeping about in fear of a bullying, highly mascu-line counterpart. If she stopped to think, she would realize that the suf-fragettes would cringe to see their flag being waved over this spiritually and emotionally corrupt relationship.

Not until Elise gains some self-confidence and begins to see herself as an individual rather than a walking socio-political statement-cum-house-keeper, and subsequently brings Pat to pay, can she break the cycle of abuse. Instead of self-nurturing, Elise has cultivated deliberate ignorance and, in fear of losing security, home, and children, is forced to turn on all who attempt to help her extricate herself from Pat's covetous and violent fist. Because the relationship is, by its very nature, supposed to be countering patriarchal abuse, the theme of psychological abuse *regardless of gender* has been entirely overlooked.

Kath, on the other hand, knows she is being emotionally abused by her mother. Frequent childhood beatings were replaced in her late teenage years by verbal lashings; then, when Kath moved away, the face-to-face attacks were replaced by searing letters and phone calls any practicing Harpy would have been proud of. To her shame, Kath, at twenty-eight, still felt reduced to the emotional stature of a small child when confronted by her mother's wrath.

However, because Kath was determined to discriminate between her mother's own complexes and the reactions she invoked in her terrified daughter, she learned how to remove herself from the toxic environment and allow a little perspective into her life. Slowly but surely, with the aid of her partner and a plethora of therapy techniques, she became able to disentangle her subjective response to her mother from her objective overview, and to adhere to the latter mentally, if not always emotionally. To achieve this involved dredging up many emotional shipwrecks, but because she was so determined to progress, she forced the details to the surface, where she was able to recompose, assess, and begin to assimilate the whole.

The three initial steps one must take to end abuse are: *conscious recognition, acquisition of self-esteem,* and *determination to fight the abuse.* Unfortunately, all are easier said than done, as these cases demonstrate. Enlightenment certainly cannot be forced. In some cases, people choose to be prisoners in order to find out the hard way the purpose of their time on this planet, convoluted as it may seem. That suffering is not a necessity is a concept still to be learned by many on this plane.

Of course, many of us are aware and willing to admit when we have been abused, particularly if it was physical as well as emotional. It may have taken place in the past, but perhaps its memory surfaces at inopportune times; for example, if the abuse was sexual, it may prohibit current sexual relations. Maybe recurrent dreams are underlining latter-day feelings of helplessness. The manifestations are countless—but in undergoing a purgative exercise such as this, at least some of the karmic mist should be lifted.

In the case of physical abuse, those who claim they would positively kill any potential encroacher or attacker are being insensitive to the millions of victims who never stood a chance. It is easy to stand back and fantasize perpetual integrity or feats of bravery and strength in a crisis; it is quite another managing them.

Although caution over one's safety is essential, there is no need to allow fear, gratuitous or otherwise, to dominate our lives. Indeed, what greater infringement could there possibly be on our liberty? Personal responsibility—not self-blame—is the key. We are all alone on this plane and it is inane to rely on other people, as so many women do on their men, for protection. Circumstances dictate that there are things we can do and things we cannot. As Kali likes to remind us, we are mortal, and though we may feel big in our little world, in many ways we are very fragile. As she also indicates, along with Durga, there are surprising reserves of strength behind the delusion of frailty. It may sound like a mixed message, but it is easily translated. *Take optimum care of yourself; be brave; be true to yourself and to the powers of justice, and in return we will take optimum care of you.*

When we enter Kali's circle we say goodbye to our precious sense of ego and are utterly humbled, as are so many of those born into her service. Most of Kali's native worshippers belong to low-caste communities in which pride is as unlikely a character trait as humility is to a Bollywood (the Hindi film industry) star in Mumbai. Kali is like death—the force that equalizes irrespective of social status or personal or borrowed power. Many who have "died" or who have had a near-death experience lose their fear of death; indeed, many look forward to the uplifting spiritual calm they feel on passing through the dimensions. Likewise, we can lose our fear of everything Kali represents once we have experienced and passed through it. Dissolution is not such a terrible thing; there are many wonders on the other side of the veil.

VISUALIZATION FOR ENDING CYCLES OF ABUSE: PART 1

Light one black, one red, and one white candle, in that order.

If music helps you visualize, play something that reminds you of the situation you are intending to recover from or terminate; if you prefer something less personal, Diamanda Galas or anything melodramatic and satanic-sounding is ideal. (However, avoid music if it will distract you; it is important that your imagination is fed rather than led astray.)

Contemplate the abuse you have undergone; the cycle you wish to break. Allow yourself to become angry and upset. The more intense your feelings, the more powerful the visualization will be.

Resolve to terminate that which is causing your grief. Steel yourself in readiness to extricate yourself from the situation, either literally or mentally (if the issue is mainly psychological or a hangover from the past).

Now, breathe in and out three times, and as you do so imagine red light filling your lungs and permeating your body. Continue to think of the scenarios that have caused you so much pain. As you do, the brightness of the red encasing you increases.

Gradually, you feel your blood being fortified by superhuman strength. It is the strength of justice, and it seems to be swelling in your body and mind, permeating every aspect of your being. You begin to feel indomitable, and as the blood pumps quickly through your veins you notice that your aura has grown spiky and is extending in ferocious points from your body.

Now, focus on the flame of the black candle and imagine it receding beneath you, so you are viewing it from an ever-increasing altitude. As you look down at it, you notice a necklace of fleshy skulls hanging down to your waist, and a skirt of severed arms about your hips.

Imagine, dancing around the black candle far below you, tiny caricatures of the people who have abused you emotionally, mentally, or physically. Concentrate on their diminutive forms until they are well established in your mind, and allow your thoughts to turn to bloodlust. This is your chance to get even.

Make your presence known to the soon-to-be victims of your retribution. As you tower above their cowering forms, swiping at them and decapitating them as a cat might batter a bluebottle, be aware of yourself as literally *above the situation*. Whatever they have done to you in the past has not cast you low but rather raised you high above them all.

Return mentally to the scene of the abuse, and *be* your new, empowered persona. Recall the moment of crisis, then turn on them as you are now. Shock them. Frighten them as they did you.

Really let yourself go. If you can, use physical actions to accompany your visualizations; this is the root of voodoo. As you launch your attack, punch the air or a pillow, or tear a pad of paper as if it were their flesh. Your power is limitless; do unto others as they did unto you. Effect your own judgment, your own retribution. Know that your actions are influencing your abusers-turned-victims astrally; there can be no doubt that with every lashing you give them their power is diminished.

Blow out the black candle, the center of their power.

In comes Kali. You look a lot like her so her grisly appearance does not frighten you; she is your sister in battle. As a matter of fact, you seem to be merging with her—you now have four arms to effect your vengeance, and a tongue made to lick up blood.

Tear your demons to pieces. They are attached to you and easily accessed through your aura . . . follow the bloody cords and rip them as if murdering some unwanted offspring. You may have bred this pestilence, it may have become embroiled with you, but you no longer want to be affiliated with it.

Kill it.

Continue in your death-dance for as long as you feel comfortable.

When you are quite satisfied that the negative entities have been sundered from your person, and you are happy with your retributive carnage, incinerate the bodies in the purifying fire of the white candle flame. Imagine yourself committing the mangled remains of your abusers to the fire of peace. When you are ready, mentally cauterize your own wounds with the white candle's light. Imagine it sealing your body and spirit to exclude further infringements on your person.

Come out of this emotional ordeal whenever you feel ready, and blow out the red candle. Return to the process whenever the mettle in your soul is rusting. Remember that justified anger is not karmically debilitating but entirely necessary. Do not feel bad about feeling bad. Kill the cycle of abuse before it kills you.

If you have been listening to music as you purge, either switch it off now or change to a soothing soundtrack; something light and fresh.

Wrap the two used candles in a piece of black cloth and take the white one, still lit, into the bathroom with you for Part II of the process.

Ending Cycles of Abuse: Part II

By the light of your remaining white candle, fill the bath with warm water. You may like to light some more white candles to brighten the bathroom as you bathe.

Light a stick of sandalwood incense and waft it around the room and over your naked body.

Now, hold a fistful of salt skyward and visualize it glowing a brilliant cleansing blue-white. Scatter it into the stream of tapwater and watch the luminescence spread to every atom of bathwater.

When the water looks a glowing white to your inner vision, step in. Immerse yourself fully in the cleansing waters, conscious of letting the unclean matter of your past dissolve and flake away as you do so. Allow the negativity you previously felt to seep out of your body and into the water, leaving you calm and relaxed. The memories of the experiences you underwent are transforming themselves into positive strengths; your body is glowing with the white fire of initiation.

Having fought in battle and emerged victorious, you may now consider yourself a warrior to be reckoned with. As you float your body in the purification bath, allow your mind to roam and survey the expanse of your experience. Feel proud of yourself for having survived when many would have fallen by the wayside.

Splash yourself with the purifying waters until no residue of your bloody confrontation remains.

Take several deep slow breaths, in and out, knowing that you have released yourself from the cycle of abuse. You have fought and won. In all future battles, you have Kali on your side. Having been there and done that, and with the goddess' assistance, you have nothing to fear. You have crossed the abyss, confronted the worst that is possible to face—you can never be vulnerable again, with this wealth of experience behind you.

Award yourself a certificate of courage, and determine never to let such a situation arise again. However, if it should, you know you could cope. Above all else, you have a sanctum of inner purity that nothing and nobody can defile.

Arise radiant from your bath when you feel ready.

As the last of the water spirals down the drainhole, carrying with it the last of your grief and fear, know yourself to be thoroughly cleansed of the past. The future is all yours now. You have passed the tests and graduated into a higher awareness. The ghouls have been conquered and your life is your playground. Resolve to enjoy it.

After extinguishing the white candle, put anything of it that remains with the red and black candles. Snap the black candle in half and say "Enemy mine, your curse has failed to taint me." Tie all the pieces together in the black cloth and bury them somewhere far away from your home.

OVERCOMING PHOBIAS

Phobias are as fascinating as they are inconvenient. The illogical impulse of terror when confronted by a spider, a feather, or a body of water tells us a great deal about our present psychology and our past lives. For example, hydrophobes are often extremely self-controlled, refusing to get drunk or "let themselves go"; likewise, they refuse to float on the waters of life. Water being symbolic of emotion, they are basically afraid of the strength of their own feelings, frightened they will be overwhelmed if they stop standing guard at the floodgates. On one level, the hydrophobe may have simply drowned in a previous incarnation (most of us have, at some point; it is when the death is particularly painful or untimely that we tend to recall it); most likely, the victim is subconsciously relating this experience to the concerns already mentioned. A repressive upbringing with a domineering mother and possible physical violence are usually the backdrops to this particular phobia.

Analysis, however, is not always the answer. Accepting that there is a reason for the fear does not necessarily dispel it; deep-rooted neuroses take time and reprogramming before they cease to be unruly. Repeating a visualization continually can, however, do much to soothe the subconscious and stem illogical fear at the source. Familiarity breeds contempt if one wills it so. It is worth interpreting phobias for their spiritual symbolism and the startling insights one may glean from these bizarre aversions, but it feels good to shed them. Nobody likes to be shackled by uncontrollable impulses; unless, of course, they are seeking attention. In most cases, however, the phobia is entirely genuine and, if you are contemplating this exercise, you clearly wish to be released from it.

A goddess is not specifically mentioned in this visualization in order to keep the process relatively simple. Instead, I use a scenario that actually occurred to me while I was in Thailand contemplating Kali. Even though she is not mentioned, the principles and events derive from her, and the experience befits the goddess' role of strength-bearer in adversity, as well as challenger of fearfulness. It is on these grounds that the following exercise has been formulated.

VISUALIZATION FOR OVERCOMING PHOBIAS

There is no need to employ deep breathing prior to this exercise. If you encounter your phobia in the street you will not have time for such tactics; best to approach it au naturel, as you would in the wild, so to speak.

Decide on who you wish to take with you on this inner journey. You can choose a friend, a partner, or an expression of your future self—the part of you not shackled by such considerations as phobias or other ailments. If you feel attuned to this Higher Self, a visualization concerning that person will be extremely positive. Whomever you choose, they will be referred to in the exercise as "X."

Also, if you have more than one phobia, decide which one you wish to deal with in this exercise. It is best to handle your fears one at a time. You can repeat this exercise another time using another phobia if you so desire.

Imagine yourself in the jungle.

You have been walking for some time, following an old mud track you hope will lead to civilization, or at least to something interesting. It is extremely hot. You are in a holiday mood, enjoying the opportunity to explore the tropical island you're visiting; you are aware of being quite a long way from your shack.

So far, you have crossed several plantations, and in one of these you passed the most enormous bull you've ever seen. Its scythe-like horns were lowered, but luckily, not in aggression. The formidable bovine was busy at its meal of luscious grass.

You are enjoying the scenery, especially in the company of X. You are chattering about the flora and fauna and wondering how likely it is to be knocked unconscious by a falling coconut.

You come to a narrow part of the track. X takes the lead; you lag a little, admiring the tropical environs. Sweat drips down your face, back, and legs. The humidity is stifling.

There is quite a big gap between the two of you now. Looking ahead, assessing your route, you are startled to notice a pit in your immediate path. Gazing in, you are horrified to behold a profusion of your phobia lying in the gap, directly between you and X.

Terrified, you gaze into the abyss, your instinct to run almost curtailed by the petrification you feel.

A noise behind you makes you turn.

The bull you passed earlier is heading your way, and at speed. You either brave the phobia-filled abyss, or end your days as a human kebab.

X, on the other side, is bidding you act with speed. They suggest you stare into their eyes as you take the leap. With the heavy thud of hooves thundering at your tail, you have very little time to make the choice. You take one last look at the seething mass of your phobia. Adrenaline coursing through your veins, you jump. It is not easy, but you have forced yourself to do it.

Behind you, the bull crashes into the pit. X embraces you in relief.

Repeat this visualization until you are thoroughly acquainted with the idea and image of the thing that scares you, and you do not hesitate to make the leap of faith. Repeat it until you know that, in real life, you would do the same thing fearlessly, bull or no bull.

MUNDANE ARCHETYPES

The Kali-character is the enfant terrible, challenging complacency in her own life and that of others, and is therefore disquieting company. She will push others to the limit for their own sakes; she forces one to fight, to prove one's mettle. People either love her or hate and fear her.

Kali never accepts emotional half-measures or cover-ups; she riles until honesty and courage are attained. Because of her excellent ability to assimilate negatives she may be unsympathetic toward those who, on attempting to absorb the darkside of their psyches, suffer emotional indigestion. She often tries to shock, to shatter the norm. Her confidence is considerable, and she finds dullards hilarious. She has a fascination with death which some consider morose; she is really fascinated by other people's reactions to this natural function of life. It may take her some time to discover the root of her interest, however.

As a child the Kali archetype is dynamic, often too feisty. She is the sort to take an uninvited bite of a hapless classmate's chocolate bar, if not the entire thing. As a teenager she enjoys fierce music and pours scorn on her peer group's proclivity toward boy bands.

Her softer side is revealed in matters of love; even her worst rage is bound by this golden cord. She commits strongly and is likely to go to any lengths to preserve a relationship she deems worthwhile. It is through friendships and relationships that she reveals her more classically feminine attributes; in these she can display remarkable self-control and kindness. However, the trait that most characterizes the Kali character is an intense lust for life in its most vivid aspects. She wants to experience the whole of the carnival, dead and alive.

TAROT CARDS

Judgement, The Tower, Death, The Devil, Ace of Swords.

Laksmi

Laksmi spreads her sails across the Hindu pantheon, stately as a ship coming into dock laden with gold, spices, and finely crafted jewels. Her cargo is burnished with a holy luster: her gifts are for the royal and priestly, the noble and devout; her stories are of enterprise and virtuous behavior.

This Empress' sons are rulers whose authority springs from diplomacy rather than force, for mounted on their gem-bedecked elephants and pungent with foreign spice-oils, they quell the peasants by presence alone, and all who see them call them demigods.

Laksmi, mild and rich as butter, sits and smiles. Blesser of brides and consecrator of marriages, she guards the cream of life, pouring it into the upheld jugs of those who please her, curdling that of those who do not.

Ghee lamps shine in her honor, attracting Laksmi's luck into the house. If her devotees are truly blessed, she will inhabit their very bodies; their faces will glow with beauty, their deepest wishes will come true.

It is Laksmi's blessing that makes of an incarnation a delicious morsel of consciousness.

THE NATURE OF LAKSMI AND HER PRACTICAL APPLICATIONS

Laksmi is depicted in the Vedas as the goddess of status, wealth, and sovereignty, which, needless to say, makes her an extremely popular deity. Her name means "sign," but she is also known by the title of *Sri*, meaning "prosperity." Her unchallenging nature (as opposed to that of, say, Kali or Durga), and the ease with which her blessing is attained mean she is easy and effective to work with.

Laksmi is appealed to by modern Hindus for *artha* (wealth and fortune), and is frequently depicted framed by golden coins and with money flowing from her palms. She has elephants as her consorts, another sign of power and majesty. Sometimes the noble beasts are showering her with water from their trunks, representing the fertility conferred by water. She is associated with light and its qualities, and candles are often lit to engender her favor. In this aspect, Laksmi usually exhibits a yellowy ghee-colored complexion and aura, denoting well-being and nourishment.

Her other gifts include *moksa*, or beauty, *kama*, which is supreme carnal pleasure, and *dharma*, or righteousness. In the case of the former two, the goddess develops a pink hue denoting compassion and femininity; when appealed to for loftier purposes such as dharmic balance, she becomes the radiant white of the cosmic intelligence itself. It is in this aspect that we recognize her sisterhood with the other goddesses, particularly with Sarasvati and Radha, who is purported to be an avatar of

Laksmi when Vishnu is incarnate as Krishna, and perceive on less specific terms the all-pervasive, motivating force behind them.

Often Laksmi sits on a lotus, in a pose indicative of transcendence of earthly ties. She is surrounded by lotus buds and blooms in various stages of development, representing the various stages of the creation of the universe. Thus we witness her in the ubiquitous role of cosmic creator; for all goddesses have a hand in the origins of human life, and Laksmi the fertility-bearer is not an exception. When she first emerges in Hindu myth she is compellingly beautiful, and she and Vishnu spend a great amount of time making love, underlining her progenitive properties.

She carries with her a pot of *amrita*, the bliss-juice of immortality churned from the seas of Indian mythology, with which she can grant kama and bestow ecstatic states. In another hand she bears a bilva fruit, unappealing both to sight and taste, but an elixir of health. The bilva symbolizes spiritual strife—moksa in its highest form. Although popularly portrayed in Indian painting as the personification of beauty, the beatitude Laksmi can grant is not merely physical.

Her other properties such as wealth and royal power, symbolized by other hands bearing such paraphernalia as a conch shell, an arrow, or golden coins, are sublimated through the influence of divine will and spiritual awareness, manifesting as a lotus blossom. Bearing this in mind, it is possible to appeal to Laksmi for meaningful wealth; that is, what we need in order to achieve our life's ambitions, plus a little more. As many New Age writers have pointed out, this is an era in which following one's heart can bring rewards of all natures, including material. The time to be coy about comfort—or guilty for it—is long-gone, compassion and generosity withstanding.

Traditionally, Laksmi's boons are sought through *vratas*, tasks of devotion usually enacted during festivals, for which the goddess will, if pleased, grant rewards. This is the same principle as saying 300 Hail Marys on one's knees to gain Christian grace; in many religions, penances and hardships are used to attract divine attention. Though Laksmi is not among their number, deities often require blood—of animals or of their devotees—to renew their ability to give, the primeval mind having construed them as such. In Hindu mythology, even demons can, and frequently do, gain incredible powers by performing gruelling feats of self-punishment and endurance; inevitably, they show their true colors once their boon has been granted, and Durga or Kali has to be brought in to sort them out. The principle indicates that no matter how bad one's past, it is never too late to curry the favor of the great ones. Because of the appealing nature of her gifts, comprising everything from large incomes to marital fidelity and fertility, Laksmi receives a great deal of devotional penance and abnegation.

As with all actions, she has an equal and opposite reaction, embodied by her sister Alaksmi. Alaksmi represents misfortune and regret, hexes, poor health, and ugliness, and can be found in icon-form in some temples, a crooked hag riding an ass. During the Dipavali festival, when demons run amok and pecuniary abandon is encouraged, images of Alaksmi may be found in some temples in place of that of her sister. At the end of the festival the unlucky crone is evicted by use of fire-torches and a cacophony of pots and pans, or she has her nose and ears broken, symbolizing the breaking of the spell. Beautiful Laksmi is reinstated and a new cycle begins. Thus she also represents new beginnings, recuperative properties, and protection from evil.

SPIRITUAL AND MATERIAL WELL-BEING: PREPARATION

For this meditation we approach Laksmi in her golden, wholesome aspect. She brings the ultimate wealth—happiness—and from this flow the props of life: food, shelter, health. She encourages us to look behind the veil and recognize that all earthly manifestations have their origins in the spiritual realms. The fruits of the earth plane come directly from the astral and causal spheres—and we influence these by our very thoughts. By channeling our desires through Laksmi we can clarify and define them, and make it easier for our positive thoughts to return to us in specific, solid form.

The following mediation involves visualizing a park, and it will help if you decide prior to the exercise what your park will look like. The scenery should reflect your state of mind. If life seems difficult to you at the moment, let it be winter. If things are looking up, choose spring. If you are already feeling pretty good, you should visualize the verdure of early summer. Dress the trees and bushes up or down accordingly, but be sure to leave plenty of room for future embellishment.

VISUALIZATION FOR SPIRITUAL AND MATERIAL WELL-BEING

Sit cross-legged on the floor or bed, take several long, deep breaths, and imagine yourself sitting in the same position in a park. You are possibly sitting beneath a peepul or banyan tree; or it may be a cool pine or a spreading oak—choose one that best befits your mood.

Before you lies a lake, its surface ruffling reflections of the sky; a few lotus leaves are floating on it.

Looking around, you notice the season.

Admire your park scene, and think about how lovely it will look at the height of its flourishing in summer, and how you too will be full of health and happiness by that time, with no material concerns to drain you.

Now, the scene becomes flat. The three-dimensionality has gone, and you realize you can peel the entire scene away like a freshly glued poster.

Catch a corner and pull it upward to reveal the brilliant yellow light behind. This light seems thick and nourishing; you can touch as well as see and smell it. Each particle glows with inner radiance, and the overall effect entrances you. You realize that there is light behind everything: an all-pervasive essence of expansive, conscious compassion.

As you think this, your original image of the park becomes superimposed on the yellowy radiance; you witness both scenes at once, and your own involvement in them. Feel the yellow aura envelop you like a blessing, protecting and sustaining you.

Now, visualize the lotus leaves flat on the lake beginning to glow. Gradually, their buds rise up; some remain in germinal state, others begin to open to reveal pink and white pointed petals, and several burst into full bloom. Of these, one is particularly large and beautiful—a giant white flower from which flow effulgent rays of yellow light, like the light you saw before. The central petals are still unfolding, holding you in happy suspense.

Slowly but definitely the petals open to reveal the stamen-like form of a ghee-colored goddess standing erect at their center. Gold coins fall in a glittering cascade around her, like a flowing golden curtain.

Laksmi wears a garland of pink lotus-flowers, and her four palms are facing you in blessing. From the lower left there falls a steady stream of newly pressed coins of the currency you use, which seem to fall into your lap until you are all but buried in them. Mentally absorb them into your aura; incorporate their weight and color into your astral body until they are no longer "visible" but you are aware of their presence. Thank Laksmi for providing you with whatever material means you may require to fulfill your ambitions.

Her upper left and right hands, meanwhile, hold lotus flowers; these flowers are white and exquisitely scented, and symbolize your transcendence of material attachments. Resolve to use the materials lent to you by the cosmic intelligence to the best of your ability, and to fulfill your own conscience.

In her right lower hand Laksmi holds a golden pot of amrita, the essence of immortality, health, and life itself.

Now, with all the power of your breath and presence, ask Laksmi to bestow on you ultimate spiritual and physical health and well-being. Even without tasting the bliss-juice, you can feel these qualities coming off of her in potent waves. The air is dense as clarified butter, but infinitely nourishing.

As the pot comes up, imagine you are swallowing a draft of its sweet liquid contents—something like celestial peach schnapps—and be sure to thank Laksmi effusively. As you do so, watch the park speed itself into a sudden height of summer; one that you know will not be prone to quarterly change. This summer is as permanent as your own fully realized and realizing potential.

Return to your room with the yellow glow still wrapped around you, and light a small yellow, white, or pink candle of thanks to Laksmi. Place it in a secure position in the window and imagine its rays attracting luck into the house, or sit over it for a while welcoming Laksmi's influence into your life.

Envision a part of Laksmi abiding with you as golden light; in your feet if you wish for luck in real estate issues; in your thighs for wealth; in your genitals for a marital blessing; in your chest if you wish for children or luck on their behalf; in your heart for wish-fulfillment; or in your facial features for inspiration and qualities of attraction. Revisit the park scene whenever you need a burst of energy, money, or faith.

MUNDANE ARCHETYPES

The Laksmi character is unquestioning of her own good fortune, taking wealth and health to be her karmic due. In adversity she is often equally stoic. Although a benefactress by nature, she can be impatient with other people's misfortune when self-induced or recurrent.

She allows herself the appearance of modernity (designer labels and contemporary clothes, for example), but is highly conventional and suspicious of the extraordinary.

The Laksmi character will pick for her friends those who are similarly well heeled, pleasant, and acceptably presented.

A strong paternal influence affects her childhood and life-decisions. She will rarely accept as her suitor one who is not handsome, rich, or both. In India, she will be caste-conscious. The Laksmi-character thinks carefully before entering into a relationship, and is by nature monogamous. Occasionally she might experiment with a partner she does not necessarily wish to marry, as long as her peer group is in approval.

The Laksmi-character is confident and at home in her body, neither arrogant nor beset by complexes. She is often of a larger build and, as long as she is not teased in early life, is happy to be robust. She looks forward to a steady, prosperous marriage blessed with children.

Laksmi's approach to religion is orthodox, and she readily accepts standard hierarchy. Her glory comes through family achievement, social status, and matronly honor. Sociologically, she makes a classic mayoress. However, she may be better at gracing the functions than changing the conditions of the town.

She is not ambitious for herself either spiritually or materially, since she already has plenty to fulfill her needs. She can lack innovative thought. She will laugh at anything unfamiliar and consider it weird, without malice but certainly with no will to comprehend. She can, however, take the abused under her wing and provide them with protection. Within her own sphere she is generous, loving, and reliable. Her faults are overconventionalism and mental laziness.

TAROT CARDS

The Empress, Queen of Pentacles, Ace of Pentacles.

RADHA

Above all else, Radha loves Krishna. But does Krishna love Radha? Such is the question that taunts her as she goes desolately about her marital duties between illicit meetings. She cares nothing for her status and wealth, for the shame and destitution that would inevitably ensue should they be discovered; she thinks only of the lowly cowherd in whose company she experiences divine love.

Radha loves Krishna. But Krishna consorts with other women; his attention is divided. Does he too long for her, does he dream of her when he is away? It is agony, the thought of him looking lovingly into the eyes of another; and at the thought of another regarding him as her own, she wants to kill. Immolation at such a time would be a blessing. Rather the searing lick of real fire than exclusion from Krishna's flaming astral aura.

O Stealer of Hearts, the sky is Krishna-blue, the earth is as red as your lips; I cannot breathe without breathing you.

The sight of herself in the mirror sickens her, her beauty wasted. Not for mortal pleasure these perfect limbs, this fathomless gaze. Music that is not his celestial flute insults her ears; all voices that are not Krishna's are like the mindless chattering of apes or the peacock's ugly screech. In Krishna's presence the feathered serpents know to hold their tongues. In Krishna's presence all things are made sacrosanct. Without him, this life is a pointless sham.

All this Krishna knows—yet he still abandons her.

He claims he loves her; he claims she is his ecstasy, and still he goes. Her tears are reciprocated doubled or tripled (Krishna always repays with interest), yet the same day she is alone with her sighs and her clouds and the pain of pretending to be normal.

If her husband knew, he would accuse her of . . . what does it matter? To Krishna's celestial love song, his words are a mosquito's whine. She must endure the illusion of separation until the cogs of good karma return her to the Krishna-blessed bower.

It does not matter.

Nothing matters, save that Radha loves Krishna, and Krishna loves Radha.

THE NATURE OF RADHA AND HER PRACTICAL APPLICATIONS

Radha is blessed with a love whose fulfillment creates cosmic consciousness and god-realization; yet she is still prone to the human failings of jealousy and depression. Her relationship also has the surprising aspect of being adulterous; surprising, that is, for a religious tract. This incongruity is reconciled when one realizes, as Radha does, that her relationship with Krishna is her life's highest purpose and as such, all obstacles between her and it, whether social, marital, or material, should indeed be hurdled. This persistence parallels that required by the devotee to realize God, and can be applied to all lofty aspirations. Therefore, an important aspect of Radha's strength is faith in her own conviction, even when it flies in the face of friends, family, and all sensible advice.

Despite the assurances of her cowherd lover, Radha spends much of the *Gitagovinda* feeling rejected and lovesick; it is her personal quest to accept that Krishna's love, metaphorical of God's, is nonexclusive. Likewise, true devotees of the divine seek to gain a nonexclusive sense of god-love—a cosmic consciousness in which the ego is dissolved. Consequently, *viraha*, or love in separation, and unconditional love, are among the gifts that Radha has to offer. Indeed, Krishna initiates often seek to emulate Radha's obsessive and all-consuming passion. As Sri Bhaktivedanta Swami Prashupada, leading light of the Krishna movement today, states: "The actual perfection of human life lies in always being *Krishna* conscious and always being aware of Krishna while performing all types of activities"; as such, Radha is a shining example of the perfection of yoga. Nothing can tempt her from her devotion. Naturally, this does not apply to everybody's lover, but the element of selflessness and absolute love remains relevant.

Just as Krishna's flute with its irresistible lure leads lost souls out of delusion and into the light, Radha's example of unconditional love can lead us closer to our divine nature.

It might be said that all human relationships are symbolic of our yearning for communion with godhead: there is no more daunting prospect than being alone in the universe. In sects of two, in familial groups, or in tribes endorsed by the religious or social proclivities of a multitude of others, humankind clings together—often inappropriately—looking for comfort, forgetful of what lies beyond the facade of actions and emotions. Just as Radha often forgot the pure source from which our positive feelings originally sprang, may we also forgive ourselves for forgetting.

Such thoughts are socially unconventional (and inconvenient), as is Radha's illicit love for Krishna. Yet the illicitness itself contributes to the strength of their union, as do the long periods of separation during which Radha is grief-stricken. Without the loss, she would not feel the gain so strongly. Unfortunately, this is one of the principles of duality through which this realm functions. Pain exists to heighten pleasure, or so the sages say. Coping with the day-to-day grievances that no philosophy can salve is one of Radha's functions as a goddess of *prema*, or selfless love for the beloved.

There was a time when the last thing women needed was a visualization for selfless love; it was simply a standard requirement of being female. Brothers, husbands, parents, and children came first, and she who did not possess the quality of selflessness to an uncompromising degree was anathema, both to herself and to society at large. In the West, however, things have changed to such an extent that selfishness in women is often considered a virtue, as are materialism and hardened careerism. This single-mindedness has been essential in tipping the balance from the rampant chauvinism of the past to a closer proximity to sexual equality, but for those of the younger generation brought up with a strong sense of individuality and ambition, it can sometimes be difficult to express one's gentler traits—the aspects of humanity, not just femininity, that have been habitually manipulated and recently discarded. This is a case of throwing the baby of spiritual transcendence out with the cleansing bathwater of challenge.

Selfless love, once the ultimate strength, is now often perceived as a weakness, but in circumstances in which one's individual integrity is not threatened, such qualities still have much to offer. This does not necessarily mean being a martyr to a partner or elderly parent in the time-honored manner. The point is to act not out of duty, but in response to an inner prompting. There are occasions when giving is called for, and when giving is right. There are also occasions when compliance to the demands of others would mean mere servility; it is up to one's own intelligence and modernity to discriminate. When it is right, Radha can help us give gracefully.

Selfless love might be required when, for example, a partner needs to broaden their horizons and progress individually—a university course, a trip abroad, a group of new (or old) friends; such things may make us doubt our position in their affections, thus inviting into our constitutions the stuttering crone Insecurity and her shrewish hand-maiden, Jealousy. The impact of these emotions can only serve to lower our self-esteem, already quite shaky in the challenging circumstances. In such situations, it is obvious that the eventual outcome will be of benefit and that the process is necessary, but a huge amount of selfless love is required to banish these baleful feelings. Perhaps we will undergo a compromise to our lifestyle while the loved one pursues the necessary course of action—their long faces certainly suggest as much.

It is under these circumstances that Radha will be ready and willing to help, if supplicated. Why go through things alone? There are thousands of entities out there whose purpose is to help bridge the gap between the mortal and the divine. Radha, queen of loving sacrifice, is but one among their number who, as a living, intelligent personality, still developing just as we are, exists in part to answer calls such as these.

APPROACHING RADHA

The first step is to resolve to meet this winsome, passionate goddess and to be infused with her capacity for uncompromising love. Radha is an infinitely attractive astral being who perfectly combines love with spirituality. She may be approached, therefore, through the chakras of the heart (green) and the third eye (purple), and as she reigns supreme in the courts of obsessive love, a sense of intense desire and appreciation is helpful in accessing her.

Before any ritual or meditation it is beneficial to take a bath. Candlelight and essential oils will help create a soft, fragrant ambience appropriate to Radha—try lotus or rose-scented bubbles, or romantic ylang-ylang or jasmine if you prefer essential oils (rose oil can be used, but tends to be very subtle in the bath).

Salt is not recommended in this particular bathing brew, as it is best to approach Radha honestly. Salt cleanses, but Radha will sympathize with the doubts and insecurities she knows so well.

LETTING GO TEMPORARILY: PREPARATION

This visualization is for those who require a quantity of selfless love to temporarily endure an unwanted compromise. Those who must abandon their desires or relationship altogether should turn to the meditation entitled Cutting the Cords.

As mentioned above, a bath will do wonders for your ability to liaise with this deity.

While in the bath, try to concentrate on the person toward whom you wish to feel selfless love. Consider why you love them, their qualities, and their endearing traits, even those failings that fill you with affectionate amusement. Try to invoke their Higher Self in your mind's eye— become aware of them as beautiful, free-flowing spirits with whom you are lucky enough to be involved. Be aware of yourself also as a loving individual with whom this being has chosen to interact for your mutual benefit, not for your mutual constriction.

Think of how lucky they are to have you in their lives, and of all the things they've done for you. Affirm that the bond between you is strong, eternal, and progressive; your very actions are proving it to be so. At worst, the visualization can only strengthen the love between you. At best, the potential is as limitless as it was when you and your friend, partner, or relative first set eyes on one another.

Visualization for Letting Go Temporarily

Once you have lulled yourself into a loving mood, sit on a cushion on the floor or bed, in lotus posture if comfortable, or cross-legged.

First, take three slow, deep breaths.

Now take three more, but as you do so, imagine your body glowing brilliant white. With each inhalation and exhalation the luminosity of your body increases.

With three more slow, deep breaths, envision a stream of electric blue light flowing into the crown of your head and surrounding your body. Feel it penetrating the violet of your third eye zone; see how its color mingles with and intensifies the radiant green of your heart-chakra, creating a turquoise area that spreads up and down your body. Feel yourself encapsulated by this vibrating turquoise light.

Listen with your inner ear. Is that a flute being played? Birdsong? Or a peacock's distant mew?

Visualize a giant lotus flower floating in the air before you. It is shut, but you can tell from the visible petals that it is very pink—a suitable color for a goddess of love. The closed bud gleams with infinite potential.

Now you find yourself at the edge of a lagoon-blue lake, watching the approach of the pink bud nestled in its bed of green. Perhaps you are sitting on a lotus leaf yourself—look down with your inner vision and see. Do not worry if your perceptions are different or even nonexistent; try to feel the approach of Radha, Krishna's favored consort, in any way you can. Everybody has different modes of perception; as the magickal adage asserts, intention is everything.

A low rumble, like distant thunder, provides a continual background to this and many other visions. It is the hum of the universal motor, the sacred syllable "Om" that provides the backbone and is the source of all creation.

Still breathing deeply and slowly, watch as the lotus flower opens.

Little by little the petals ruffle outward; in the center, you know the goddess Radha abides.

Compassion permeates the air like a pink-orange sunset; emotions run high when this deity is abroad. There is a turquoise sheen on the lotus leaves similar to the color of your aura; allow yourself to be influenced by the resplendent colors of your vision, just as Radha will respond to her vision of you.

The petals continue to unfurl.

Consider the nature of Radha as you contemplate her emergence from the center of the flower. She too has been forced to let her beloved leave her; mentally make appeal to her compassion. She too has had to transcend personal desire for greater good; offer her the image of your own situation and she will recognize it. She is emerging now, attracted by the familiarity of the plea.

Continue to breathe in and out in blue and turquoise, and allow your spirit to be refreshed by the all-pervading "Om"; you feel a thrill of anticipation as the innermost petals gradually reveal the luminous deity.

First you see her resplendent headdress of gold, emerald, and ruby shimmering at the uppermost tip of the center petals.

Then Radha's face becomes visible: the blood-red bindi between the eyebrows, her enchanting and sympathetic eyes, the golden nose-ring set elaborately with gemstones, her full smiling lips, and lustrous dark hair falling down her back. Be aware of her as half-Krishna, just as Krishna is half-Radha. She is, indeed, his bliss-component.

When the goddess has arisen fully in your inner vision, surrounding you with a profound sense of beauty and love (if you have "seen" nothing, then this is the thing to look for, the hallmark of Radha's presence), ask her to bestow on you some of her nectar of transcendence. In her slender hand she holds a golden vase; she lifts it toward you.

Mentally explain to the goddess your predicament, which is similar to her own when Krishna had to leave her to fulfill his role as avatar; and request that you, like she, have the faith to gracefully withstand the illusion of separation. Affirm that, in this instance, you desire the strength to put another's well-being before your own.

Watch as Radha raises the vase high above your head and baptizes you with the golden liquid it contains.

Take a moment to fully appreciate the import of this blessing.

Your wish has been granted; Radha will help you in your cause. Connect your third eye with Radha's by envisioning a line of light extending from the middle of your forehead to the center of hers, and feel her sublime acceptance, devotion, and love permeating your aura and falling down your spine in great cleansing waterfalls. You are now bestowed with the strength necessary to surmount any obstacles in the course of your love for the individual concerned.

If Radha does not bless you with the heavenly unction, or if you feel a great resistance to your plea—at worst, if all of these visual cues run in reverse in your mind despite your calm state of being—then it is time to reconsider your plan of action. Perhaps you have sacrificed your own desires for those of another once too often. Perhaps this level of giving is inappropriate to you, in this particular set of circumstances. You cannot force a blessing, and if you fail to receive one, try to accept the higher wisdom inherent in the denial—a wisdom that springs from your inner self and from the goddess petitioned. If a decision is required, try one of the other exercises in the book, such as the weighing-up visualization channeled through Maat.

Either way, when you are ready, thank Radha for the wisdom received, and return slowly to your position on the floor or bed.

Remember that, in your coming to terms with the situation, it is not just the other party who is being progressed, but you also.

Letting Go Permanently: Cutting the Cords

This is a tricky one in anybody's book. If someone we love abandons us for whatever reason, it can often be tempting to turn to Kali or Durga for revenge rather than to Radha for loving transcendence, so consider yourself already halfway to heaven if you have chosen this path.

The following visualization is for those who wish to free themselves, as well as the reciprocal party, from a relationship or situation that has become stultified or damaging. When progression along separate paths is painful but necessary, it is time to cut the mundane cords that fetter you both.

Cutting the Cords: Preparation

There are various psychological preparations for this exercise that come naturally to most of us, such as throwing out (or burning) old letters and memorabilia, removing obsolete photographs from their frames, possibly rearranging our furniture, and altering the house. If the relationship was that of lover, then new arrangements and color schemes in the bedroom can be particularly effective.

However, if you are looking to totally eradicate the wayward party from your life, then Radha may not be the goddess for you. What she has to offer is not amnesia, but a positive appreciation of the past relationship. You can expect to experience a feeling of elevation as you realize that the interaction between you and your previous partner or situation was, however disguised, a blessing for both of you. The ability to move forward in the knowledge that you are both fulfilling your personal destinies will then follow. On some levels, you will be more bonded with the person than you were previously, as Radha brings understanding on a soul-level—the most personal of bonds. The mode of interaction will no longer be restrictive or negative, however. Like

Sarasvati, Radha is something of a New Age therapy goddess. Of course, all deities have a healing aspect and may be employed as such, but some are more suited to contemporary ideals than others.

With Radha, you are allowed your faults and failings and offered the ability to improve yourself through effort, self-love, and love of others. The cords you will be cutting are not the cords of memory but those of ego-attachment to the person in question. On these grounds, then, may the goddess be approached.

A salt bath is recommended prior to this visualization; not because Radha requires you to be purified, but because it will relieve you of a lot of unnecessary psychic baggage. As you place the fistful of salt in the water, visualize it glowing blue-white like luminous washing powder, and imagine it having formidable cleansing properties. The grime this substance will be removing, however, is not tricky collar grease, but deeply ingrained astral dirt—that is, the residue of all your negative feelings for and confrontations with the person you are letting go.

As you enter the warm water, watch with your mind's eye as the muck flakes off your body and dissolves. What a relief! By the end of this bath your aura will be radiant white, something it has not looked or felt for what seems like ages. You will leave your former tensions, black knots of jealousy, and barbs of spiteful thoughts in the water to be purified by the salt. White candles are recommended to aid this process. A sandalwood or jasmine joss stick will also help put you in the right mood to contact Radha and make this positive step into the future.

VISUALIZATION FOR CUTTING THE CORDS

Settle yourself comfortably, either cross-legged or lying down if you prefer (though be sure not to fall asleep).

Now take three slow, deep breaths.

Begin the meditation by imagining yourself surrounded by deep blue light.

Gradually, it fades hue by hue into brilliant white.

Continue to breathe slowly and deeply; feel the white light streaming through the top of your head, at the crown chakra, and allow some of it to flow out of your solar plexus. You may notice it exiting this region in specific lines like cords—if you glance at their ends you might be able to perceive a specific person or symbol. These are the astral-emotional ties that bind you karmically as well as psychologically to a person. You are looking for those that relate to your ex-partner or the person or situation with which you are splitting. Chances are, they will not be hard to find, most likely being the strongest and grubbiest-looking of the lot, though not necessarily. If the situation is painful, they may even look jagged or bloody. Use your intuition to tell you which cords relate to whom.

If you so desire, allow yourself a little time to study these fascinating relics of your emotional life. This is a good opportunity to throw white light at all of your emotional ties; do so until they look clean and radiant to you, and the unpleasant matter no longer returns.

Now, take three very deep preparatory breaths, in and out; you are steeling yourself to accept that what you had hoped for has not come to fruition. You must cut the cords for both your sakes. It is not going to be easy, but you are resolved to act in the highest interest of all concerned. You are effectively liberating yourself from a self-chosen bondage.

Holding the bonds you wish to break in your mind's eye, visualize yourself wandering through a forested wilderness in search of Radha, in whom you know you will find solace. Now is a good time to let your hurt, grief, and disappointment surface; do not be afraid to feel the sorrow that is natural when saying goodbye to your former dreams.

Seek out Radha among the tangled thickets and shady bowers—you know she's around here somewhere. She will be wearing white, the color of abnegation of earthly values, and her smile will be wiser and sadder than her former girlish glee. She will probably be glowing, like moonlight, with a pearlescent aura broken only by the brilliant red of her bindi. Call to her as you wander the lonely forest.

Continue to breathe the white light, deeply in and deeply out, and remain holding the ties you wish to break; you spot what looks like a silver shadow flitting between two trunks. The trunks are silhouetted, along with their branches, by the light flowing from the fleeting lady.

Drawing closer, you perceive the fabulously bright, fawn-like form of Radha.

She will understand your predicament without explanation, but feel free to explain if you wish. Perhaps it will help clarify matters in your own mind.

Hold out to her the cords you wish to break.

With your hands extended, proffering the cords unique to you and the person you are letting go, take three extremely deep inhalations and exhalations, while mentally requesting Radha to help you in this cause. Then watch as she raises her silver cleaver and brings it down at your solar plexus. She is so quick and efficient that there is no mess, and the cords snap neatly back into you. Somewhere else, the other person's cords are doing the same thing.

Feel the many new directions you are free to explore—be aware of the new full scope of your potential. Know that the past can never be taken from you, but that the future is all your own. Allow Radha to bestow on you some of her pure silver-white light, and bring it back with you when you re-enter your earthly room. Breathe the silver in and out and become accustomed to the new sensation of cleanliness and liberation around the bottom of your ribcage. Now that you feel relaxed and refreshed, return to your everyday life, cacooning yourself in Radha's silver aura whenever you need a psychic shower.

If Radha did not respond to your request, there may be more to learn from the situation, even if the lessons are painful. Try to maintain the overview that you hopefully experienced during this exercise, and carry that wisdom back into the situation you feel has become obsolete. Keep repeating this exercise—there may only be a little way to go before you complete this particular experience. When the time is ripe, Radha will come forward to help you continue on your individual path.

Mundane Archetypes

Many intelligent, artistic types display Radha traits in adolescence. The Radha-character is obsessive and impractical, but shows remarkable tenacity in her fixations, so much so that she often proves her critics wrong by evincing from her calling something genuinely unique and worthwhile.

She is deeply religious, either literally or in relationships; she will make a living deity of her spiritual partner, once that person is found. She seeks salvation through ecstatic union, which could make her extremely sexually active. She craves extraordinary qualities in all she encounters; when her life lacks the components of intensity and transcendence she becomes depressed and lethargic. Creativity may ensue, most likely in the form of paintings and poetry.

The Radha archetype's moods swing wildly. She takes great pains to conceal her unusual nature, and though she may be arrogant in early life, she will later, if fulfilled, soften herself to an inconspicuous paragon of some kind of virtue, either religious or marital.

Cult interests will characterize her inner life. She will care nothing for cynics or conventionalists, perceiving them as transient expressions of delusion. Others will consider her a misguided dreamer. She is like the Fool of the Tarot, happily following the rainbow-bubble of her astral vision along a cliff-top while the dog of convention yaps an unheeded warning at her feet.

If any other than the chosen try to follow her, she will become possessive of her knowledge and eventually wish to push them off the precipice. If another has a better bubble and a better cliff-top, she may be jealous, even outraged. She is proud of her inner life and her individuality, though she may not flaunt it.

When separated from her dream by another's realism or by uncontrollable circumstance, she is inconsolable.

Her capacity for devotional love is exceeded only by her determination to give it, for it is through this that the Radha archetype finds self-fulfillment.

TAROT CARDS

The Lovers, The Hanged Man, The Fool.

EGYPTIAN GODDESSES

Isis

He was attracted by my green wings and the crescent moon upon my forehead.

He loved my magic; it did not scare him, it entranced.

He feared I would bewitch him, but I did not. All that he did, he did of his own free will.

Of course, we knew one another from long ago, but there can always be new beginnings, new lights in which to behold the soul. And so we fell in love like two who had never met before, and we were very happy.

Day turned to night in the lover's bower.

My moon, so recently so full, cycled around to black. Our shadow-selves began to play, reversing our emotions, deconstructing from the top the patterns we had established.

My other brother hatched a cunning plan. He had always been jealous of my husband, intent on taking his place and dispatching him to a miserable end.

So he made a shadow-play to fool my love, to lead him on a merry dance in circles of entrapment.

My husband became confused and fell into a casket of despair, which was soon set adrift on the fast-flowing river, leading far away from me.

I mourned, cut off my hair, refused my food. My magick lost its power because my grief was stronger than my self-belief.

For infinite days and infinite nights I scoured the world for the remnants of my hapless lover. I became a kite, soaring high above the homes of happier folk, my grief eating at my heart like a vulture's beak. I could not believe I had allowed a chink in my psychic armor big enough to admit the serpents of destruction. All that I ever wanted had been forfeited by this oversight.

Eventually, I found him.

A tree had grown around his body; it seemed that he was made of wood.

I used all that remained of my sorceress' arts to recompose my husband to a semblance of his former glory, but part of him was missing, the part that guaranteed our future together.

So I built him a phallus of wood, and I took his seed through its mediation.

Still deep in grief, I resolved that my offspring should avenge his father's premature demise. Light versus darkness until the dark is conquered, evermore until the karmic debt is paid.

Where do I belong? In between the two; a creature of both. With my companion phantoms I abide between the divine and earthly realms, a contact point for those on either side.

I am known by many names: Isis, Great Mother, The White Goddess; but the name that I prefer is Mercy, for I shall always give it.

Through pain and the making of human mistakes I have learned compassion. And so shall I forever remain a willing intercessor and granter of aid to those in need on the stormy seas of life and death alike.

The Nature of Isis and Her Practical Applications

Isis is one of the oldest godforms in existence; her history spans thousands of years of active worship. Consequently, she is bestowed with many aspects, each one a reflection of the needs and attitudes of those supplicating her at the time. Isis' functions range from those of a basic goddess of providence, the succoring and fertility-bringing Great Mother, to those of civilizing the people and protecting women and children by encouraging marriage and monogamous commitment. She also presides over the intellectual complexities of ritual magick. It is unsurprising then that in modern magickal practices Isis often represents all goddesses from all cultures rolled into one. She is indeed the supreme female deity, her functional scope as wide as her sky-embracing, soul-protecting wingspan.

It is in Hathor that Isis' nurturing qualities are best illustrated. The divine cow is permeated with Isis' presence, as are all female deities, despite their different functions. Cattle are also relevant to Isis in her capacity as civilizer, being symbols of agriculture. Isis is often shown with cow's horns when suckling Horus, or Hathor appears with full cow-visage, resting the young solar god on her knee. This bovine symbology perfectly exemplifies the perpetual beneficence of motherhood.

Another position shared by these goddesses is that of "mothering" the pharaoh, the living Horus, and providing him with divine nourishment. Isis, whose hieroglyph is that of a high-backed throne, was considered quite literally to provide the lap in which the royal backside might place itself. Sitting thus, the pharaoh received both Isis' mother-love and the effects of her wisdom. Consequently, he was invulnerable.

Like many Egyptian deities, Isis is intimately connected with the rising of the Nile and flooding of the Nile valley, until recently so essential to those living in her native country. She is associated with the star Sirius, also known as Sothis or the Dog Star, whose rising heralded (or, it was thought, brought about) the inundation of the valley, and she is associated with the fertility and growth that ensued.

As loyal sister and wife of Osiris, and loving mother of Horus, Isis was the obvious deity to whom to appeal in the cause of fidelity and the protection of the homestead. She is said to have devised marriage contracts, and is protectoress of sacred love. It is through Isis that lovers are reunited in new incarnations, particularly those who have undergone a soul-bonding ceremony in their previous lives together.

Isis' vivifying qualities are represented by her ability to become pregnant by Osiris' dead body, and by her gathering and subsequent resuscitation of most of his organs. Even when deep in mourning she motivates herself to action; she does not allow her grief to interfere with the possibility of her love for Osiris becoming his redemption, which, indeed, it does. Likewise, she nurtures the helpless, crippled aspect of Horus/Harpocrates into strength and rectitude. Isis' domestic qualities bring spinning, weaving, and cookery into her domain in addition to healing, sex, and conception. She is the best goddess to whom to appeal in the cause of stable and spiritual love, as the exercise on finding one's ideal partner indicates.

Isis is the High Priestess of the Egyptian pantheon; some would argue, of all the pantheons. Having tricked her uncle Ra, once the supreme solar deity, into telling her his names (i.e., the vibrational key to his essence), she procured formidable occult energies for her own use. Many of her skills went into helping Osiris in his continual battles with Seth, his seethingly jealous brother and polar opposite. Along with his female counterpart Sekhmet, to whom he is married spiritually if not actually (his wife being Nephthys), Seth represents the dark side while Osiris and Isis represent light, love, and forgiveness. Likewise, with Egypt herself as the metaphor, Isis is the good land, Osiris the fertilizing water, and Seth the desert. Osiris' myth, of course, became integrated into that of another solar deity, Jesus, and Isis' into Mary. Both pietás end in the salvation of light via resurrection.

Isis is also a goddess who opens the inner eye, revealing the mystery behind the veil of delusional mundanity. An in-depth example and partial explanation of this is given in Dion Fortune's classic novel *Moon Magic* and its prequel *The Sea Priestess*.

Isis is the moon goddess and counterpart to solar Osiris, who, owing to his propensity to move below the horizon after sunset, also rules over the Underworld. Isis knows the secrets of the dead and living alike; she knows our obsessions and fantasies; she is the guardian of dreams. She is said to unite with humans as they sleep, bestowing the healing energies and life-giving light required for sustenance. In Hinduism this subconscious influx of prana is controlled by Durga. By sleeping in Isis' temple, devotees hoped to gain guidance and help in dreams. This is the shadow-side of her role as mother and nurturer, protectoress of women and marriages. She epitomizes feminine mystique and quiet power.

With her long dark hair, often depicted in a Cleopatra cut, and lunar disc headdress, Isis presents a striking figure, but hers is the art of understatement, of subtlety, and she is almost always taciturn. She looks after her own, and, in the habit of strong women, exhibits favoritism and disdain in a sometimes unpredictable manner; her moods often go well beyond the logical.

Isis' gifts do not come cheap. She will demand a sacrifice, and it will be something dear to her prospective devotee—their social life, a beloved partner whose presence is not conducive to her plans, or simply one's complacency. Isis is as harsh as she is mysterious, but her rewards are indubitable.

The word Isis (originally *Iussaset* or *Aset*) is associated with several meanings, mainly *throne* (later, of the pharaoh), *seat*, and *nature*, and the wonders of nature are among her domain. She is often depicted wearing a throne-shaped crown.

Isis presides over the tides of the ocean and its unplumbed depths, symbolic of the subconscious, and, therefore, over other lunar-influenced systems such as the menstrual cycle. Many plants have lunar correspondences—rosemary, for example—and these are most sacred to Isis.

ENCOUNTERING ISIS: PREPARATION

A good time to access Isis is on the evening of a full moon, at twilight. Any between stage such as dusk or very early dawn will do, the former being preferable. It is best by the sea on the night of a full, clear moon or, if you can't manage outside, in your makeshift temple nearing midnight. In all cases, the contact is enhanced by feeling excited or high-strung, so don't worry about those neuroses. They are, indeed, often helpful in attracting the cosmic healers.

A little pomp and ceremony will befit you to encounter this ultimate mistress of ritual magick. You could, for example, wear a special cloak and invoke the quarters prior to the visualization. Covenesque paraphernalia (chalices, athames or ritual daggers, or statues of the god and goddess, for example) will help reconfirm your rapport with the goddess; however, these are psychological props and not necessities. As with the preparations for all of the visualizations, do what feels right to you.

Burning a little rosemary or myrrh, or using jasmine, sandalwood, or lotus in your bath will help you get on the Isian wavelength. An aromatic, candlelit soak with a little salt in the water for purification will help prior to the visualizations. (See the beginning of each exercise for specific bathing recipes.)

INCREASED POWERS OF INTUITION: PREPARATION

For channeling this aspect of Isis, a lunar bath prior to the visualization will be helpful. You may leave moonstones (if you have some) and a little salt in cold water for thirty minutes and add to the bath water; this will endow it with the vibrational qualities of this gem. A little milk can be added, and you can gather mother of pearl and silvery objects on the side of the bath to admire by candlelight as you soak. Isis or moon incense with rosemary overtones will be of benefit. Candles may be white, royal blue, purple, or black.

Envision the bath glowing with silvery pearlescent light. As you step into it, feel yourself entering the liminal zones between worlds; a place inhabited by beings conversant in the material and spiritual worlds alike. Feel the realities mixing, the similarity between shadows and solids, dog and wolf, the living and the dead. Watch their half-recognized forms move about the room as you lie in the warm water. This is the real twilight zone, right here in your bathroom.

If you have some purple solarized water (see Introduction), add it to the moon water when you have mentally established its lunar properties. As you do so, imagine the bath flooding with purple light and energizing the purple of your third eye area. Watch it glow until it illuminates the room. Be aware of stepping into silvery purple water as you enter the bath.

As you soak, center your energy on your forehead, in the area above the bridge of the nose, and between the eyebrows. Purify yourself for as long as you need, and imagine the white light of the salt in the water dissolving your negative feelings and any mundane fatigue and preoccupations you may be harboring. Enjoy the shapes of the steam and incense, and the shadows thrown by the objects in the candlelight. Let your imagination loose as you lie in your vibrant bath.

When you emerge, see your body glowing pearly white with a brilliant purple forehead.

You are now prepared for a powerful goddess visualization.

Visualization for Increased Powers of Intuition

Sit cross-legged before a white or purple candle, at twilight if possible. To make sure the candle doesn't blow out when you exhale, place it at a distance from you.

Take several deep, slow breaths, and hold the air in your lungs for five seconds at a time; wait five seconds before you inhale again. As you do so, you are charging your astral body up for flight, and making yourself more visible to Isis. Imagine your body glowing brighter with every breath, and feel the new pranic energy tingling in your body. Don't forget to keep the third eye area drenched in purple light.

Now, visualize the silver orb of Isis' headdress. Notice the special quality of the astral silver, so pure that it can pass effortlessly between dimensions. Draw back a little to admire the crescent moon-boat beneath it. Is it on her forehead or not? It is difficult to tell. Now that you look a little closer, it almost seems to be painted onto cloth.

Moving back, the full figure comes into view: Isis kneeling, her wings outstretched, her face set in an enigmatic smile; a picture on a veil. Behind it, you know the goddess abides, but you will have to penetrate the veil to find her.

Taking a few more pranic breaths, resolve to acquire the energy to find her, wherever she might be. You need to increase your powers of intuition and realign your mundane self with your Higher Self, and who better to guide you in this than the mistress of magick herself? Call to Isis as you begin to mentally move through the veil. Imagine yourself being propelled forward as you do so. Use your will power to pass between realities.

Behind the veil, you find water. It is black and white; an ocean at night. The darkness of the water meets the darkness of the sky, and both are eternally deep; the water's surface is delineated by the flashing of silver wavelets far beneath you. You are travelling very fast, in lotus posture, between the deep dark sea and the blue-black sky in which a single silver orb is hanging.

Eventually you see a vast throne of white marble rising out of the water. A pillar stands on both sides of the throne, the left one black and the right white, and seated at its center is the glowingly visible slender form of a veiled woman.

As you approach, you are endowed with a strong sensation of vibrancy and awe. You travel toward her sandaled feet, and prostrate yourself at the feet of the goddess, mentally making your plea.

She tells you to arise and you hover before this larger-than-life, white-clad figure, admiring the fluidity of her form, suggestively concealed, at once ancient and youthful.

You will probably have personal impressions at this point that cannot be predicted. Be sure to memorize as much as you can for further analysis and use.

Still, you have not seen the face; just a teasing hint of black hair at the edges of the veil. Just as you are wondering how to glimpse behind it, Isis raises her right hand and taps you sharply on the forehead between the eyebrows.

As Isis touches you, you receive an image of import. A message is delivered in the goddess' resonant voice. Listen carefully to the words chosen, however bizarre they may seem, and write them down, along with any other impressions you receive. If you do not wish to break your concentration by making notes now, be sure to memorize what is said, and record it as soon as you emerge from your meditation.

You may receive confirmation of your life path or a cryptic criticism; you may receive a clue to your future, or advice about your progression. Whatever is said, do not forget that your purpose is to increase your intuitive capacity, so let it be known that this is the purpose of your "visit."

You may also be told whether you will ever penetrate the veils.

If you receive nothing, or a negative image, return to your room and resolve to try again when the time is right for you. It may be that increased powers of intuition or interest in psychic studies are inappropriate to you at this point in time.

If, however, the response is positive, continue your internal dialogue for as long as you feel inclined. Once you have established a rapport with Isis on this fundamental level it will be easier to access her at any time of day or night, and to slip into the part of your personality that allows you to contact higher intelligences.

And, of course, the more you practice and enhance your intuition and inner vision, the stronger they will be.

VISUALIZATION FOR MAGICKAL ABILITY

Magickal ability is the art of directed will combined with strong visualization. Therefore, the best way to increase it is to practice concentration techniques; the old classic of staring exclusively at an orange for ten minutes can work wonders. Alternately, you could think of something that provokes a strong inner reaction, perhaps something you really long for, and try formulating your feelings into a golden net and "capturing" it. However, if you prefer something more ritualistic, this may be the visualization for you.

Arise from your ritual bath empowered, but in the humble knowledge that you are a mere neophyte (no matter how far you have come down the magickal path) to the supreme High Priestess you are about to encounter. You know you have a long way to go, but you are confident of your ability to achieve formidable occult prowess. This is partly because you know you are prepared to put in the effort.

Take several deep breaths; envision yourself breathing in light as you do so. Feel the light penetrating every cell of your physical body and every atom of your astral one.

Flex your psychic muscles by extending your aura to the periphery of the room, making it glow as brightly as you can, and then withdrawing it again.

Now, stimulate your chakras one by one by concentrating on each in turn, starting at the base chakra. Make the red discus spin and, as it does, feel yourself attuned to your primal self. Then work your way up the orange intestinal area, the yellow solar plexus, the green heart, the blue of the throat, and the purple pineal chakra. Finally, as you concentrate on the golden-white discus at the top of your head, feel yourself assimilating the cosmic energy that infiltrates all aspects of being.

If you like, you can practice turning these vertical discs into horizontal discs and then throw them around like Frisbees. A frivolous exercise like this is quite a refresher, particularly when dealing with a deity as solemn as Isis. Be sure to reincorporate your auric Frisbees into your energy system at the end of the session.

Now that you have limbered up, imagine yourself flying at high speed through astral space. You may see anything at this point; landscapes, strange geometric shapes, symbols—it's down to your own intuition and inner vision.

Whatever you see, feel the sensation of flying. Hear the whirring of your chakras, like propellers driving you forward. Keep your ultimate goal in your mind's eye; a deity who embodies magickal ability and in whose very presence your own aura and ability will rise to new heights.

Eventually, you reach the throne. It sits at the water's edge like that of the Tarot's Queen of Cups, and on both sides there is a pillar, the left black and the right white. There are offerings on the steps before it: pomegranates, votive candles, and mummified animals, mainly ibis birds and cats.

The Priestess is unveiled and very beautiful in the moonlight.

Her heavily kohled eyes assess you with an air of nonchalance. Now it is up to you to prove your worth.

So, shine as brightly as you can; present your soul and your will to learn the magickal craft and see if she accepts it. Watch her hands. A small gesture may indicate acceptance or rejection.

If she rejects you, return to your room and resolve to practice until you reach an acceptable level. Alternately, it may be the wrong time in your life for such endeavors; be sure to interpret the response in the light of your personal circumstances, and be as realistic as possible about it. Perhaps you were not respectful enough, or perhaps you need to work more on the feminine side of your psyche. Only you will know what the real cause is.

If the Isis-figure does accept you, move forward with an air of quiet humility and positive aspiration. Mentally communicate to her the object of your quest, and be sure to add (and feel) that you will use your abilities to the greater good of humanity. There is no point in applying to Isis if your ultimate aim is selfish, manipulative, or harmful power; she, like most godforms, is unwilling to cooperate with plaintiffs such as these. If the aim, however, is self-development, healing arts, or spiritual progression, she is likely to respond favorably.

Now that you are in Isis' presence, see how she reacts to you. She may touch some part of your astral body, which indicates the need to develop it, or she may even bestow instant healing; she might shapeshift and take you on a journey. Whatever it is, go with it for as long as you feel confident. The Wiccan rede "Perfect Love and Perfect Trust" is particularly applicable to Isis. She will reward those who put their entire faith in her; do not forget, she is Nature. Like Kali in her most fearful aspect, she will never betray those who deliver themselves unquestioningly into her hands, though as a final test of faith, *she may produce the illusion of doing so.*

Make sure you request, plainly and clearly, the augmentation of the psychic powers you already possess. Compare yourself to Isis prior to her empowerment, and confirm that you too will use your abilities in a positive manner. As you depart Isis' domain, she may hand you a package or talisman. Be sure to keep a hold of it and feel it in your hands on your return.

It is difficult to describe this astral trip as it will be very different in the case of each individual. Whatever you experience, stay with it until you feel inwardly fulfilled, and when you return to the room, consciously bring your new power with you. Much of it may be in the form of confidence and resolve.

You are now ready to write down and interpret the experiences you have just had, possibly in a Book of Shadows. The symbolic aspects of your visualization are likely to be important signposts to you on the magickal path.

VISUALIZATION FOR FINDING YOUR IDEAL LONG-TERM PARTNER: PREPARATION

This visualization is best performed when you have tried the conventional methods of attaining a suitable counterpart and are feeling disappointed and even depressed by your apparent inability to do so. Consequently, it is intended for those who are single rather than those who are in a relationship, though, of course, it is up to the reader's discretion whether they perform it when involved. However, the visualization should not be used to try to turn any particular person into your long-term partner. The idea is to attract to you a person who already harbors the specific qualities you seek, and not to alter another's personality.

Before charging into a long-term situation, it might be worth remembering that life experience is an essential ingredient to any relationship these days, particularly if it is to have a spiritual dimension; long gone are the days of premature monogamy and subsequent self-stultification in the name of partnership. However, if a younger person finds themselves attracted to this visualization, it may be right for them at the time. Obviously, it must be acknowledged that some souls are older than others, and that experience cannot be represented by an annually changing number. So, use your integrity to decide whether a visualization with such permanent repercussions is really what you want, no matter how old or young you might be.

If you feel somewhat battered and bruised by life; if you've really been there and done that and have had it up to the back teeth with learning processes and formative experiences and being a one-person band, then this could help answer your prayers.

If possible, the following preparations should be performed at twilight on the night of a full moon, with the visualization following directly afterward.

For a magickal visualization of this nature, it is important to pamper yourself prior to the exercise.

Take a long hot candlelit bath with an herbal infusion; add a few drops of fragrant essential oil such as rose or geranium. Bubbles in the bath are appropriate both to Aphrodite, whose properties are relevant to your cause, and to Isis Pelagia, the Lady of the Waves. This is an oceanic aspect of Isis you will be dipping into later. If you like, treat yourself to a glass of wine (or drink of your preference) while in the bath, and listen to some music that makes you think of the sort of person you would like to have as a partner.

Allow yourself to daydream about your ideal partner—how they might look, how they will treat you, the type of conversations you will enjoy together. If you want to share children or animals, imagine them too. Try to get as accurate an image as possible of what you want from your future, without imagining any one person in particular.

Observe the shadows that flicker around the bathroom as you lie swathed in steam. They may seem insubstantial, but they are created by solids. Your imaginings are also a real reflection of your future, which can be crafted into anything you want. Resolve to create your own reality in the style of your choosing. The materials are out there. All you need to do is hone in on them.

Arise from the bath when you feel attractive and confident, and perform your toilette as if you were about to meet the partner of your dreams. When you smell and look gorgeous, retire to the room in which you plan to perform the visualization.

Note: The state of mind induced in this visualization is used to facilitate a particular archetypal response, and in no way represents the author's personal opinion regarding celibacy.

Visualization for Finding Your Ideal Long-term Partner

Light three small candles of green, blue, and white, respectively.

As you light them, be aware of the flames as a focus on the astral plane, attracting the type of partner you wish for.

Take several deep breaths of light, in and out, but hold the light in your body, and resolve to enhance their energies by investing your own will power into the flames, whose light crosses the dimensions and sends a clear signal into the emotional worlds.

Sit cross-legged before them and envision yourself flying through the air, very fast over the twilit trees and houses, then over the fields that lead to the sea.

Notice the full moon, hanging huge and low in the sky, a surreal white-silver orb imprinted with the face of the goddess. Tell her your woes as you travel toward the ocean. Do not be afraid to have a good moan; you've been through the mill on this simple quest, and for what? It is not that much to ask, a decent partner and a happy home life, is it? Why can't it all be as straightforward as this flight?

As you journey toward the silver and black ocean's edge, you grow more and more depressed about your lot. The black of the sea and sky seems to reflect the black of your mood, and the cliff-tops you are rapidly approaching look like the edge of the world, the land's very end.

You come to a halt at the cliffs and gently descend over them, into the frothing white foam at the black ocean's edge.

The water is very deep and probably quite perilous, but you don't care. Without that special person in your life, what is there to live for anyway?

In your despair the water begins to look quite inviting. You put one foot in, and a wave instantly engulfs you. You struggle to the surface, but another one is on you now. Seven times you rise gasping to the surface, and seven times you are submerged in the black salt water.

Exhausted, you focus on the full moon hanging over the water and address Isis, Queen of Heaven.

At this point, project the images you had in the bath of your ideal partner and the life you would share together, and mentally compare them to your current circumstances. Ask Isis to work on your behalf, to lift you from your misery and grant you what you know to be simple and possible.

Address her as Queen of all Women and Initiator of Marriage Contracts; appeal to her as Patroness of Marital Fidelity and Family Life. Tell her that you feel you have lost your Osiris—or Nephthys—she will understand your yearning. Appeal to her as a woman who knows how it feels to be bereft of one's other half.

Now watch as Isis arises from the sea. She is vast and impossibly beautiful; her eyes are veiled but perceptibly shining with compassion. Twin serpents entwine on her headdress; between them is a silver crescent moon. A merciful smile plays about her ravishingly red lips; and in her hand she bears aloft a cornucopia.

Around her slender waist she wears a knotted girdle. If you wish to have children in the future, the powers of this girdle are of particular relevance to you. You could appeal to the Great Enchantress with this ultimate aim in mind.

As with most of these visualizations, you are likely to have personal experiences that are impossible to predict here. Spend as much time as you need with Isis, letting your emotions go, purging any negative hang-overs you may have from previous experiences. Be sure to stay by the water's edge in the moonlight until you are feeling positive and strong and, of course, do not forget to continually request the granting of your wish for an ideal partner.

When you have very strongly projected your previous daydreams in the direction of Isis' forehead, along with your request for its coming to pass in the material world, and are feeling confident and uplifted, you are ready to return.

Thank the goddess for her help, and promise to do your very best by what is granted to you as a result.

Fly back over the fields, housing estates, and roads until you reach the window of your room. See yourself sitting before the candles, and reenter your body.

Open your eyes safe in the knowledge that everything has been done to bring about your heart's desire. Every time you look at the moon, you will strengthen the spell. Every time you see the ocean, you will be reconfirming your purity, your ability to move on emotionally.

Try to feel as if you have met that person already, as if you are already in love. With the "in love" aura wrapped around you, you will prove extra-attractive to everyone, including your future partner. Be aware that you are drawing them to you with the strength and confidence of your belief, and that you are consequently *making your own reality*.

Having created this magickal atmosphere, you can have a lot of fun simply observing who comes into your life at this point and the situations that arise. As all such circumstances are metaphorical of inner truth, you can learn a great deal by analyzing and interpreting them.

Most importantly, enjoy yourself. You have done all that you can to attract your counterpart, and fate may be encouraged, but it certainly cannot be forced. The most conducive thing you can do at this juncture is to remain happy and relaxed.

Now, let Nature take her course.

Mundane Archetypes

As a girl, the modern Isis has much of the Persephone about her. She never quite sheds that sense of separateness, which may give her the air of being aloof; others consider her shy and socially inept.

Her strong inner world of emotion and spirituality is always of paramount importance to the Isis archetype; her interest in the outside world is primarily in nature and the astral manifestations of physical situations. In other words, she beholds the sacred in nature and always looks "into" people rather than at them.

Coupled with her quietness, this can make her an unnerving companion, and the "down to earth" may consider her pretentious or neurotic. She can, indeed, be both, for her yearning to return to a pure, disembodied state naturally attracts her to occult studies and lateral subjects, and their overspill into her often unsupported life can cause immense tension between conscious and subconscious levels and urges.

Sexually, she is obsessive and soul-searching; psychologically, prone to deep depression and feelings of grief and sadness, often inexplicable to her conscious mind. The typical Isis is prone to terrible mood swings over which she has very little control. Only self-expressive creativity and the support of other women can help assuage her emotional confusion, but these friends must be utterly genuine. The loss of a trusted one is one of the worst kicks in the teeth to the Isis archetype.

She has great psychic potential, but can be too solemn in her application. Later in life she will appreciate a laugh en route to *samadhi*, but in the meantime the jovial will seem to her irrelevant and, indeed, irreverent. Her main relaxation will be in the form of creativity, gardening, and herbalism; today, possibly aromatherapy and metaphysical interests, and the company of trusted friends and animals.

The Isis-type is affectionate and inwardly loyal, but can be relentless in pursuit of her spiritual goals. Though warm on the surface, she can be persuaded by "higher understanding" to sacrifice that which is dearest to her—and then she is as cold as ice.

She is interested in reincarnation, mythology, and the healing arts, and is usually flanked by cats. She is the classic Wiccan woman or spiritually-inclined wife and mother. She is intense, quiet, and dark, and fiercely protective of her own. She would go to the end of the world for a loved one. She is retrospective, sometimes depressive, and believes in burning brightly when inspired. Laughter and sunlight are useful aides in normalizing her . . . too much moonlight and she turns into Hecate.

Tarot Cards

The High Priestess, The Moon, The World.

Nephthys

In the nebulous light of the eventide she loses herself once again to the realms of imagination.

She sees herself as she might have been, as she might yet be: a queen among women, lady of the house, her beautifully decorated palace swarming with congratulatory consorts.

Her future sons. All the creativity of Sekhmet without the gall. All the rich fecundity of Hathor without the boredom. The qualities of Isis.

Isis will be calling around soon, prising her from the grim reality of her circumstance. Together they will fly to Isis' home, bright with tapestries and fragrant as an herb garden, to play with the infant Horus, growing stronger and more golden by the day.

Of course, this house will be the first to suffer when he reaches maturity, but Isis will see her right. About her husband Seth, she does not care. She blames him for her unfulfilling spectral life, her sense of limbo.

She welcomes these uncertain lights, these concealing shades, and the hours when nothing can be done. It is the working hours she hates, the light that focuses on her inaction, making her feel pointless and guilty. There must be more to it than this.

Small things distract her. She paints, she scribes a message to a friend. Sullen but tinged with hope, she waits.

What is Isis doing now?

Not only can she embalm herself with the memories of a thousand nights with Osiris, brightest of the gods, but she has the best magick, the best infant, the most illuminating shadow-sister in the worlds. If her own life is a void, she can at least use it to throw Isis into relief. Vicarious fame is not such a bad thing, and better, she deems, than infamy.

Taking heart, she lights the lamp and awaits her beautiful friend and sister. They are made of the same soul-substance, indubitably. The evening star is risen; soon Isis as the morning star will bring her dawn.

And then will they be balanced and inseparable; infinitely bound by spice-pungent funerary tresses of immortal experience.

THE NATURE OF NEPHTHYS AND HER PRACTICAL APPLICATIONS

Nephthys is Isis' sister and Seth's wife. Married to the god of the desert, she is unable to conceive by him, establishing her position as deity of the unmanifest, where as Isis is goddess of fertility and growth.

However, Nephthys is unhappy with this role and determines to become pregnant by Osiris. Consequently, she disguises herself as Isis and seduces her sister's husband. By this act of deception she conceives Anubis, the jackal-headed god of divination.

Shortly afterward, Seth succeeds in dispatching his hated brother Osiris to an untimely end in a casket on the Nile. Isis, wild with grief, is approached by her guilty sister, who fears for the life of her unborn child. Isis, ever-merciful, helps Nephthys hide Anubis in the Underworld, and together the two sisters seek Osiris. Thus, Nephthys is Isis' accomplice and fellow healer and resuscitator of the murdered king.

In many respects, Nephthys is Isis' shadow, echoing and underlining Isis' various roles as protector and healer. On coffins and in depictions of Rites of the Dead, she appears opposite Isis mourning over the body of the deceased, the "Osiris" of the situation, while casting her expansive wings over them in protection. Likewise did she mourn with Isis over their lost-and-found lover, sometimes taking the form of a kite in her grief.

Though married to the god of evil, Nephthys bears him no allegiance. Indeed, most of her actions attempt to rectify what the hand of Seth has defiled. She compliments Isis' role by counterbalancing it; where Isis is the dawn, Nephthys is dusk; where Isis is the new moon, Nephthys is the old; where Isis is fecund, Nephthys is menstrual: the pharaoh was said to be comprised of her magickal fluid.

Often, the two are barely distinguishable from one another. Nephthys cleaves to her powerful sister's side, shapeshifting to avoid her own unpleasant husband and aiding and abetting Isis in her perpetual fight against the darkside.

Nephthys is, therefore, a suitable deity to approach for the purpose of putting wrongs to right. She is especially appropriate when a faulty judgment or mistake on our part has led to a rift in a friendship; perhaps trust has been betrayed or a relationship vilified. If you feel you have committed a wrongful action and wish to put it right, the following visualization should help.

Visualization for Making Amends

The best time to approach Nephthys is at twilight on a night of a dark moon.

First, think of all the traits you dislike about yourself and that you feel have caused the current situation. Imagine them encapsulated in a black sarcophagus.

Now envision yourself in your most positive light, glowing with all the good qualities you know you possess. This image also takes the form of a sarcophagus, but this time it is golden.

The two figures molded from your essence seem to be taking on a life of their own. You see them standing side by side on the bank of a swift-flowing river, slowly becoming animate. The black sarcophagus, now more of a living corpse, turns toward your golden self and pushes it into the river. Very quickly it is borne downstream.

You have a choice: You can either stand by and witness all your virtues being wasted, allowing yourself to be taken over by your darkside, or you can try to redeem the situation.

Call upon Nephthys, sister of Isis and her fellow healer, to help you now. Watch as she appears above you, a beautiful bird with a wingspan so vast that it seems like the sky itself. Will her to descend.

When Nephthys has landed, attach yourself to her by envisioning a line of light between your third eye and hers, and ask her to help you find your qualities again.

Nephthys lifts you up and bears you over the bright ribbon of river until you spot your golden body bobbing up and down below. Descend and reclaim it. As it clambers on board, reassimilate it into your soul.

The task is not over yet, however. There is still the black sarcophagus, container of all the traits you despise in yourself, to deal with.

Nephthys returns you to the starting point. Elevated above your negative self, you feel liberated, freed of trivial concerns, petty jealousies, and all other emotions that exacerbated the situation in the first place. Your darkside, once so powerful, looks feeble from up here.

As you think this, Nephthys swoops down and bears you within arm's length of the black container. Use all your strength and determination to shove or kick it into the water.

The sarcophagus opens with the impact, and the black body it contains begins to unravel. The funerary bandages, known in old times as "tresses of Nephthys," fan out in the water like matted strands of filthy hair undergoing a long-required wash, or so it seems from your newly regained aerial vantage-point.

As the past is borne away, you feel a tremendous weight being lifted from you. The water is fast and soon inundates the splitting sarcophagus, purifying and transforming its putrid contents. They are being scattered on the currents, turned to silt and rubble. Before very long, there is nothing left to see.

Silently, Nephthys glides to the ground and allows you to dismount.

Your aura is shining with a golden luster and you feel relaxed and happy.

Breathe deeply in and out, expanding and enhancing this golden aura, until Nephthys departs. She will only leave you when you are fully healed.

If you have hurt someone else in the situation you are amending, send them an apology on a tide of this golden energy. Send them all your will to heal them—all the love and affection you have ever amassed for them as fellow travellers on the earth plane. Keep pouring this healing light from yourself into them until you really feel them absorbing it at the other end.

Once you have finished, if possible, try to make amends on the physical plane too. If your apology is not accepted, try not to get angry. You do not want to start generating negative energies just when you have freed yourself of them.

While talking or writing to the person concerned, keep visualizing this vivid golden light of cosmic forgiveness. You are able to forgive them because you have blessed yourself with forgiveness also. You know how difficult it can be to be strong, and how easy it is sometimes to be swept away by the strong currents of emotion.

Thank Nephthys and repeat the exercise whenever you feel the unworthy side of your nature taking control. Try to maintain the golden, light-filled self at all times, and send the dark thoughts downstream, particularly when they threaten to interfere with a friendship or relationship again. It is not worth giving into them, for emotion is fleeting while repercussions can resound through the ages. Make amends before it is too late.

MUNDANE ARCHETYPES

The Nephthys character is well-meaning but easily led. Her lack of self-confidence can lead to misplaced loyalty, such as that for a selfish friend in childhood or an unsavory partner in adult life. She is likely to defy those who have her welfare at heart for those who do not but who offer a more desirable short-term prospect.

Her relationship with mother and sisters is uneasy, particularly if she has a sister or friend close in age but surpassing her in beauty, in which case everything of theirs will seem better and more desirable to her than her own. This deep-seated resentment will either result in self-punishment (eating disorders or inferiority complexes) or in calculated revenge on the sister or friend, such as interfering with her love life through trickery. If she resists this impulse, she may apotheosize the woman concerned, copying her hair, clothes, and preferences, and aiming to be just like her.

In partnerships she is often clingy; consequently, she needs someone with time and energy to devote to her. She will rebuke the idea of conventional marriage and children, but it is through these (or any "belonging" situation) that she will eventually find happiness.

Nephthys is secretly lonely and confused; she is always on the lookout for salvation but not wishing to be too obvious about it. She has an ongoing dilemma between the order and disorder toward which she is alternately drawn. She is creative but undisciplined. She is likely to fall in with Persephone, but will later face the dilemma of her adult Isian friends being more successful than she is.

Nephthys continually compares herself and her situation to that of others, but often relies on fate to change things for her. A frequent complaint is, "It's not fair." Durga-types can be a positive influence on her as long as they avoid dominating her; Laksmi and Radha can provide healthy friendships. However, if she falls in with the neurotic, she will swiftly adopt their neuroses as her own; likewise, her own fears can be contagious. It is imperative for the Nephthys-character to be with those who have her best interest at heart; she is easily molded and just as easily broken.

TAROT CARD
The Star.

HATHOR

Hathor shakes her sistrum to chase away bad spirits; here, everything is safe. A walled garden; a sanctuary from evil. Children play insulated from harm, enfolded in her mother-love.

Ribbons of scent unravel on the breeze: flowers and honey, freshly baked cakes, and rich dairy foods promise pleasure in futurity.

Hathor rattles her sistrum, creating rhythmic music for the small children to dance to.

Her heavy cow's head, long-lashed and smooth of line, nods in mild approval of the scene. Brown eyes reflect no sentiment, just a simple natural warmth and the will to gently protect.

Her expression is opaque as milk; pure mystery of the mother-goddess.

The red-brown earth is rich as chocolate cake, and even difficulties here are made palatable. Hathor has designed her domain to delight.

Plants and vegetables of all shades of green flow from their carefully nurtured furrows and beds, graced by flowers and butterflies of entrancing color.

Frothy orchard trees grow at the base of one giant sycamore—Lady Hathor's den.

Here she comes to consider those from whom life has been taken; here she brings foodstuffs and gifts for the untimely dead. Nobody who supplicates Hathor will go without; she makes it a point of honor to give whenever asked.

Beauty belongs to her, and it is her will to share it. In return, she asks only that her protégés be equally generous of self, and that they too offer practical help to those in need.

Need is anathema to Hathor: she would eradicate it if only the gods would permit. Her rivals continually evoke imbalanced desire in humankind to tip the scales she is evening out.

Still, Hathor and her kind will give and suckle and fortify and cushion and nurture until it is proved that the milk of kindness can never run dry.

Milk is a better substance than blood, in Lady Hathor's spellbook; for blood can augur death while milk means life.

Thus, in the very end, she hopes to prove her loving point.

THE NATURE OF HATHOR AND HER PRACTICAL APPLICATIONS

Hathor is one of the oldest Egyptian deities; she is sometimes represented as a woman wearing the horns of a cow on her head, between which rests a solar disc, or cow's ears. However, she is more often to be found as a chimera goddess with the body of a human female and the entire head and neck of a cow. Cattle were revered in ancient Egypt for the same reason they are sacred in Hindu belief: for their unquestioning beneficence. They provide us with endless supplies of milk, the symbol of motherhood, and their providence is unconditional, like a mother's love. Hathor presides over conception and childbirth, and is primarily a goddess of women. She is, however, patroness of the pharaoh, and was considered to sustain him with her divine nourishment, just as she suckled Horus in his infancy. In accessing the Hathor within, we can tap into the eternally compassionate and unquestioningly loyal side of our natures.

Another name for Hathor is "Mother of Light," an appellation that underlines her life-giving properties. It was she who gave the souls of the dead the sustenance they required beyond the grave, so that they might live on and eventually return to be reborn. As a counsel of seven cows she determined the incarnational lessons of each soul and the circumstances required to facilitate them. She often appears as the Lady of the Sycamore Tree; the tree is said to have surrounded Osiris' body when it was eventually washed to shore. Many Egyptian coffins were made of sycamore in respect of this connection—a wood associated through Hathor and Isis with the properties of resurrection.

In the typical Egyptian manner, Hathor is both the daughter and the wife of Ra, the supreme solar deity and onetime master of magic (until Isis excelled him). Together, they produce an aspect of Horus—that of his diurnal regeneration symbolized by the rising and setting of the sun. In other texts Hathor is the wife of Horus, his parentage being that of Isis and Osiris. As the son of the latter, other of Horus' traits are emphasized: those of personality and spiritual development. Hathor is connected with the physical dimension of the god, and is mistress of growth and its limits.

Just as the pharaoh became the living Horus, the queen became an incarnation of Hathor. Again, she functions as both his mother and his lover. It has been conjectured that in performing both of these roles,

Hathor symbolically transcends all sexuality; but it cannot be ignored that Egyptian mythology, and indeed its history, is replete with incestuous relationships.

A surprising aspect of this generally benevolent goddess is her transformation into Sekhmet. The latter is, in fact, another godform and has been treated as such in this book; however, the connection between the two is worthy of note. Mythologically speaking, Hathor becomes the "Eye of Ra" and watches the transgressions of mortals from a solar vantage point. When roused by their vile behavior she transforms into Sekhmet, the bloodthirsty lioness whose wrath can only be assuaged by alcohol. The deities may be separate today, but their previous interplay indicates how deep still waters can run, and how far a tranquil personality can go when pushed. It is possible that her rape by Seth contributes to this dimension of her personality. Some of the Sekhmet traits remain in the mundane Hathor archetype. The divine Hathor is, however, the antithesis of Sekhmet.

Hathor's personal history is conversely devoid of complexity; though she may be coupled with other goddesses such as Nut and Isis, as an individual deity she exudes simplicity. She is, one could almost say, the fact of life, as well as its sustainer. She is eminently suited to long-term projects and can help us bring our ideas to fruition.

Many of us experience moods in which we feel suddenly inspired toward some definite goal, whether it be writing a novel, taking a university course, or bringing a child into the world. We usually feel strongly about it for a while, often long enough to initiate the scheme; but how often does the inspiration die in infancy? We are left with a few chapters lying in the dust under the bed, a lot of boring work we don't want to be bothered with, or a lifestyle whose compromise we resent. It isn't that we've made the wrong choice or committed ourselves in the heat of the moment, it's that we've lost track of the original inspirational plan. We have failed to nurture the seed we have sown.

It is ourselves we are letting down when we fail to maintain our dreams. This is a very understandable and very common stumbling block; mundanity is often a stronger force than insight. However, it would be much easier and more positive for us if we could be consistent in our application of self; and Hathor, the most stable and giving figure in the Egyptian pantheon, can help us with that.

APPROACHING HATHOR: PREPARATION

Unlike many godforms, to become properly attuned to Hathor it is important to be well earthed. She is indeed a very "down to earth" goddess; not high-minded and convoluted like, for example, Isis. A good meal, a simple bath or shower, and a nice cup of tea will put you in a suitable frame of mind to meet this goddess of beneficence.

Presumably, you have decided what it is you want to nurture. Make sure it is something of a viable nature—if it is a difficult quest, but something you really wish to attain, fine; but if it is totally illogical and lacking in practical foundation, Hathor will laugh you off. If you have decided that your scheme is definitely within the realms of possibility, it is time to present your case to this kind and obdurate deity.

There is no need for breathing exercises or auric aerobics prior to this visualization; they will only put you in an overly-mystical frame of mind. Instead, think of the most matriarchal middle-aged woman you know; not the battle-axe variety, but the strong, stable sort who makes sure she protects her own (usually, her family). These women are sometimes lacking in imagination, and do not suffer fools gladly (i.e., those with unusual or airy inclinations, such as high-flying spiritual ideals!), but do not be duped. Hathor women are far from slow. They demonstrate a shrewd intelligence, particularly when it comes to money. They can be the steerers of the course of their often more creative, dreamy partners, and very successful captains of large family ships. They provide the foundations on which their more expressive offspring flourish.

Encountering Hathor will not deaden your creativity, but will help you provide a more stable base from which your creativity can reach new heights. Obviously, the more earthed you wish to be, the more you should meditate on this most solid of archetypal women.

VISUALIZATION FOR NURTURING A PROJECT

Approach this visualization in a frank and determined frame of mind.

You know what you want to do, but be sensible—you want to ensure that you have the power to endure in your endeavor.

Hathor is standing in a kitchen, tending to numerous pots on the stove. Children's voices can be heard in the next room and outside, talking and laughing.

The smell of baking bread permeates the room. Outside, the window branches hang heavy with apples ripening in the sun; flowers overflow their beds. You can see a beautifully maintained vegetable garden in the foreground. The house is filled with an atmosphere of well-being.

Hathor herself has the body of a stout human woman, representing her higher intelligence and sublime productivity, but her head and shoulders are those of a cow. A glow is visible on her cheeks. She seems very human, but blessed with a tranquillity that people rarely know. Her eyes are superficially bovine—certainly imperturbable—but in their reddish-brown depths there is a spark of sharp intelligence. It is intelligence in reserve, however.

Hathor glows with a deep yellow aura and halo. From her flows astral sustenance as well as physical well-being; she delivers a promise of a bright, safe future.

Try to stabilize your own astral body and imagine yourself with your feet planted firmly in Hathor's green garden; your roots extend down from the soles deep into the earth. Feel the power of the earth flowing up into your body, coursing through your veins.

Now, envision your plan as a small plant or shrub.

Hathor sees you in the garden and comes out to greet you; she wipes her hands on her apron as she emerges.

Stand planted firmly opposite this chimerical goddess. Feel the change in your vibrational rate as it slows to a steady, rudimentary beat.

Speak to her mentally in any way you feel inclined, and see how she responds. In the event that the response is unfavorable, go away and reconsider your project. Perhaps you can reformat your request into something more acceptable to this practical deity.

Now, still envisioning your project as a sapling, admire Hathor's garden with its fertile soil and flourishing greenery; communicate your appreciation to her as you do so. Again, listen for any comments and feedback you may get. They may prove useful regarding the concept in hand.

Look again at your young plant and consider how well it would do if installed in Hathor's verdant garden.

Take as long as you need to explain your cause; ask Hathor if you may plant it here. If she assents, you are halfway to success already.

Envelop your plant in the yellowy aura you have developed in emulation of Hathor's. Send energy to its base and plant it in the soil. Watch as it takes root; the deeper they go, the more definite a place it has in futurity.

Extend your aura and water your plant in whatever way suits you; a watering can or a sudden shower—whatever you prefer—and send it your devotion. Promise to tend to it every day, and to make practical moves in the outside world to bring it to the height of its manifestation.

Ask Hathor to tend to it while you are away in the material world. While she babysits your dreamchild, you can create the channels to bring it into being.

To really ensure success, visit your "plant" every day (morning is best); nurture it and watch it grow. Sometimes it might seem germinal, in which case you need to pump more energy into it. At other times, it will reflect your effort by appearing leafy and lustrous. Make sure that every time you visit it, you leave it larger than it was when you arrived; then your dreams will surely come to fruition.

MUNDANE ARCHETYPES

The modern Hathor is usually of homely physique and tends to mother her friends, especially males. She often resents more glamorous women, befriending them on the surface and using her influence to malign them behind their backs. This is because she herself is essentially monogamous and is aware of other women as potential interlopers on her happiness.

The Hathor woman's unthreatening aura and nurturing qualities make her a popular friend to the sort of men she secretly desires—pretty boys with tricky natures and a wide range of interests, love or otherwise. However, she is unlikely to capture one as a partner except through money or status; in the event that she does, she will soon become pregnant, as, indeed, she will wish to in any reasonably secure relationship.

In youth she may be found with those who live on the edge, taking it all in her slightly cynical stride, while inwardly wishing for nothing more adventurous than marriage and children. Indeed, she makes an excellent wife and mother to those who do not set their psychodynamic sights too high: she is proud of her normality compared to that of, say, the Persephone-type, channeling all of her attentions into her immediate family and their physical needs.

The Hathor woman is supremely capable, often exuding a superhuman calm in times of trauma. She excels at providing those in her favor with all the creature comforts they require, particularly during periods of recuperation. She is often a wonderful chef.

Once married, the modern Hathor will choose for her friends other Hathor-types, jealously guarding her domain from "predatory" females. Despite her sometimes frumpy appearance, she is sensuous and sexually playful within a secure relationship—raunchy even. If, however, she is unsure of her partner's devotion, she will either participate for the sake of an easy life, or sex will stop altogether.

Though hospitable, generous, and excellent with children (both literal and metaphorical), she can be claustrophobically ordinary with her partner and merciless with women of greater mystery. Her best therapies are transcendental meditation and experiences of loss, both of which can lend her greater insight and, thus, greater tolerance.

TAROT CARDS

The Empress, Queen of Pentacles.

Maat

Sobriety is my purpose and my will.

No braggart drunk on delusion can alter my word, though with petty force and unjust laws they try; for in the very definition of my word is the physical realm made manifest.

Those prayers touch me that are pure of motive; to the roar of the ego I am deaf. I am not, like children borne of flesh, easily influenced. I am Cosmic Justice, and all shall know my eternal truth regardless of their hierarchical position.

Said the lost ones, "Mother, we are caught up in a nightmare and all we see seems real; Mother, shatter this illusion we do not understand, but the knives are real and they make us bleed real blood."

Let nothing taint your vision of a balanced world; in me, the whole world is made even.

"Some people are mad, Mother. They inflict injustice as if it were a righteous thing to do. They spread lies, and cast in depravity they lean against the scales of justice and tip them down."

Where is your faith, child?

"Too long have the bright ones burned in the darkness; our resources are used up. Sometimes our souls are like ashes, self-cremated in the cause of perpetuating inner vision. Mother Maat, why do you allow the thieves of righteousness to inhabit the halls of existence?"

Self-pity does not become the Servants of the Light.

Your rectitude is its own reward, though there may be others in the end.

See how, even on your level, there are bright pockets of justice stitched into the rough fabric of your lives? Imagine, then, the radiance of those found in the brighter material of the astral and spiritual planes! Do not forget, we see all, though every soul you know may be blind. None walks immune, and every heart will be judged according to the eternal laws of truth.

We do not test beyond your means of endurance, so in hardship be honored; it indicates true fortitude of soul.

All shall be balanced and all shall be made even.

This is my promise and my purpose and my will.

Present to me the cause of your crying out and I will stem it at the source if its waters are contaminated.

Remember, the darkness is as sacred as the light, and both are necessary composites for the formulation of a day.

Trust me, for I am as inevitable as the dawn; as logical as algebra. I am the judge and the equalizer and the cosmic conclusion of all action.

I will not let you down.

THE NATURE OF MAAT AND HER PRACTICAL APPLICATIONS

Maat, or Mayet, is the goddess of justice, against whose cosmic feather-weight all hearts are weighed on death. If one has led a good life, the scales will balance, but if they tip, one's heart (i.e., essence) is eaten by the monster Ammut, a chimera from the realms of chaos. Whether the scales tip up or down is unclear; one would expect the bad heart to outweigh the feather through the weight of sin, but some sources indicate that the feather of Maat grows heavier if the organ is characterized by deceit. In this instance, the feather outweighs the heart. Personally, I have always construed the feather of Maat as being as light as a clear conscience would feel in the circumstance of judgment and, therefore, as being outweighed by the guilt-laden heart. For the purposes of this book, I have maintained the latter standpoint.

In either instance, imbalance with the feather points to incongruence with the principles of Maat. Just as a gluttonous or poor diet will eventually destroy the physical body, spiritual annihilation is the consequence natural to the Egyptian mind for acting in opposition to cosmic order. It is not so much a punishment as a mathematical certainty. Maat measures the spiritual vitamin-level of each life, thus determining its longevity. There are numerous criteria involved in this process, from internal and external behavior to the repercussions of actions committed on the earth plane. The balance of the psyche is also paramount; the anima and animus, as we call them today, must be in cooperative working condition. In this era, in which we progress from the more traditional Age of Osiris, Maat's area of special involvement includes guarding the newly developing balance between male and female forces on the external, as well as internal, planes.

Balance, indeed, is the key to Maat's mystery. In geographical terms, she represents the unity of Upper and Lower Egypt, the fertile land and the desert. She also indicates the equipoise between mundane individuality and the Higher Self with its ensuing cosmic overview. She is sometimes referred to as *Double Maat* in respect of this unifying aspect.

Maat is the principle of divinity and righteousness, without whom all deteriorates into evil. The gods themselves are said to "live by Maat." Indeed, the breath of light that confers their divinity is the essence of which Maat herself is exclusively made. She is, by her very nature, just and true; any psychological taints such as egoism, greed, or jealousy are anathema to her.

In the negative affirmation of the soul after death, Egyptians were asked to quantify the state of the heart by answering specific questions pertaining to their conduct on earth. Questions as to whether one had lied, stolen, or nurtured envy were typical of the inquisition.

However, it was the final question that could tip the scales of this matter of conscience and extricate them from the waiting jaws of Ammut. The individual was asked whether there was anyone on earth who was glad they had been born. Even if they are guilty on every other count, they could be redeemed if able to answer this question with conviction. Indeed, clarity of conscience rather than lack of wrong action seemed to be the key to immortality; if one's motivations were right, the heart balanced against the feather.

Maat is as kind as she is just; theoretically, the role model of the pharaoh himself. Indeed, in his hand the pharaoh held an effigy of the seated Maat, an echo of his own position on the throne.

Maat's consorts in the Underworld are Anubis and Osiris, and she is mythologically married to Thoth, who shares her qualities of truth and integrity. Ancient Egyptians were urged to "Speak Maat, do Maat!" Morality and the goddess' name were eponymous.

Connected with her spiritual purity is Maat's association with abstinence. Illicit sex or sexual excess, and overindulgence in food and intoxicants are particularly repugnant to her. As in many scriptures, notably Hindu and latter-day Christian, only that which purifies the system belongs in the rightfully ordered world of spiritual integrity. Conversely, she is linked with fasting; indeed, the quality of lightness is integral to Maat. Both spiritual or physical gluttony will make her scales tip downward and threaten the longevity of the heart and soul.

Many of the principles of Maat, and of the philosophical heights of Egyptian justice, are illustrated in Joan Grant's novels, particularly *Eyes of Horus* (reprinted by Ariel Press). Grant's novels provide an absorbing insight into ancient Egypt with a firsthand narrative; Grant purports to write from "far memory."

Maat, as judge of karmic repercussions, determines whose soul returns to earth, whose lingers in the demiworlds, and whose is consigned to primordial chaos and destroyed. When relieved of her duties in the Underworld, she is said to ride the solar barque during its diurnal journey across the sky. Of course, Maat's divine essence is not confined to any one place at a time. She is equated with reality, and pervades all things at all times.

However, it is not so much the goddess that concerns us here as her weighing equipment—the ubiquitous Libran scales of justice.

A major problem with decision-making is obtaining an objective overview. Ephemeral thoughts and emotions often destroy our capacity to see a situation with clarity—particularly in affairs of the heart, Maat's speciality. The sort of situations in which these visualizations can be particularly helpful are those represented by the Lovers card in the Tarot—choices and potential paths that will take us away from that to which we have become accustomed, or any decision that will have long-term repercussions.

Maat is the goddess of truth. Some philosophies hold that by speaking the truth one gains the ability to manifest all words spoken from the heart. Maat, therefore, also represents the godlike capacity to create on the material planes through will alone. As such, she represents a formidable magickal ability. Certainly, the most powerful magick has its foundations in truth, which makes it unshakable in the winds of change. Truth exists; lies are built on the ever-shifting sands of emotion.

ENCOUNTERING MAAT: PREPARATION

As Maat is a goddess of moderate abstinence, it will be beneficial to undergo a small fast for a day or two before approaching her. Basic guidelines are included in the Magickal Diet and Exercise section.

Alternately, you could make another sacrifice prior to the visualization; for instance, you could stop smoking or refuse alcohol.

If you normally eat meat, it is definitely best to forego it for as long as you feel able. One of the principles of Maat is vegetarianism.

A salt bath is a good idea before this visualization—concentrate on washing yourself clean of superficial preferences and immediate concerns.

An incense such as sandalwood or Libra mix (or, if you can find or make it, Maat) will be a beneficial accompaniment.

Noon, when the forces of light and darkness are in equilibrium, is a good time to connect with Maat; a waxing moon half-full or more will also aid the visualization.

VISUALIZATION FOR MAKING BALANCED DECISIONS

Decide on a simple but appropriate symbol for each of the situations between which you are choosing; you could, for example, use a square to represent the life to which you are accustomed, and a triangle for more aspirational pursuits. We are going to keep this visualization basic for clarity's sake. Chances are, you are already confused and too much symbolic paraphernalia will be far from helpful.

Take several deep, white breaths. Imagine the luminous white air infiltrating your bodies, starting at the core of your physical one and emanating outward to the peripheries of your etheric and astral body (for the purposes of this exercise, about seven feet from your skin in every direction). As you breathe out, concentrate on expelling from your body all subjectivity and superficial angst or emotion—inhale light, exhale confusion.

When you feel slightly spacey and your mind is reasonably blank, visualize Maat's balancing scales. They are large and sturdy, but inordinately sensitive.

Now, put your symbols in the pans, one on both sides, and see what happens. If you have more than two symbols to weigh, use the lightest of the last pair to counterbalance the new symbol.

If the symbols balance, there is nothing to choose between the options—do what you like. If one symbol crashes to the ground or is very heavy, it is a bad idea, inspired by the wrong motives. The lighter the symbol, the better the choice. If you have nothing to weigh your idea against, use the final symbol recommended—that of the white ostrich feather of Maat.

To finalize any decision process, weigh the symbol against Maat's own symbolic tool of judgment (the feather). Feel the atmosphere of antiquity caught in the fronds and sacred strands of the feather; see how particles of light adhere to it as a whole. This seemingly innocuous item has sent a thousand souls plummeting into the gullet of Ammut, and dispatched a million more to stellar life and immortality.

If your symbol and the feather of Maat balance out equally, all is well and good. If your choice is lighter than the feather, you have made a decision based on higher values; it is a worthy path. If, however, your decision raises the feather above it, you should forget it; it is a morally or psychologically corrupt choice that will bring eventual regret.

Within a few minutes you will have made a decision approved by your Higher Self, who has, of course, longer-term vision than your mundane self. It is now down to your personal discrimination whether you follow it or not.

MUNDANE ARCHETYPES

Like Iris, Maat is more of a function than a personality. She cannot be defined on mundane terms as she is the principle of right thinking and right action. From this, we may conclude that those who lead a wholesome life defined by these principles are representative of Maat's qualities, while the spiritually slovenly are her antithesis.

TAROT CARDS

Judgement, Justice, Temperance.

SEKHMET

Sekhmet sits in silver skirt, tended to by loving sycophants. Only the most beautiful people are allowed into her court of favor, where wit hisses like a flail and poetry is poured forth like a libation to pleasure. Together, she and the favored ones, the favorites known to all, observe the pandrogynous throng and its invited participants. No entry without a card.

Air-kisses fill the room like a flock of low-flying twittering birds.

Sekhmet sits and smiles in perfect poise, inviolate. Her scepter, shaped like a cobra, spits light, mesmerizing, confirming her power.

Pouting lips and glittering vestments declare the comforting perpetuity of the superficial. The smell of artificial scent and ambivalent pheromones grows thicker as the chimerical throng heats up, loosens up, and limbers up, leaving the outside world in the realms of fantasy. And all, it seems, for her exquisite entertainment.

Sekhmet smiles over her glass of hypertoxic punch into the wave of hermaphroditic splendor, teasing. Many respond.

Blithely, her gaze skims the aesthete's assembly line of male and female animae as it passes, wondering whose soul to suck tonight. The depravities of which she is capable in pursuit of pleasure and experience are a delight to contemplate; a delicious pocket of cream on a bland sea of milk.

Such is life in the palace of shifting personae, the land of the shaman and shapeshifter.

When Sekhmet is bored, all who cannot sustain her intrigue vanish in a searing flame of disdain. She skims their essence from the ether and redecorates the rooms of her mind, which is her palace of astral wonder; and from this spring new combinations and processes.

The paint of her magickal art is always wet, for Sekhmet changes her creations by the moment. Each spark of light in her slant-eyed head is captured and remolded in her mind, and then made manifest.

Such is the potential of the lioness who is one of the Great Ones.

THE NATURE OF SEKHMET AND HER PRACTICAL APPLICATIONS

Sekhmet was originally cast as upholder of cosmic order, or the will of Ra, in a similar role to that of Durga. However, at some point her fearsome aspect became the pronounced trait in lieu of her divine rectitude; retribution was replaced by gratuitous gore, and she came to symbolize the dark forces of Seth and to be worshipped in conjunction with him. As a sexual goddess associated with heat, the connection may have arisen through Seth's affiliation with the South, and powers of fire and the sun at its most destructive. Sekhmet presided over sorcery and harmful magick; Joan Grant's novel *Eyes of Horus* provides a vivid description of her worship at the height of its depravity.

In her more positive aspect, this lioness-headed deity depicts the qualities of protection, healing, grace, and a keen intelligence. Her sharp senses are especially honed to detect any threat to her own; she is a particularly patriotic deity. She was often prayed to for destruction of enemies, particularly the Nubian tribes, and her weapons included a fire-tongued cobra and the Seth-like power to parch. She is endowed with searing insight. Majestic in black basalt, she is undemonstrative about her quiet, unquestionable strength.

Sekhmet is associated with Ptah and Ra, sometimes appearing in the form of a *ureaus* on the brow of the latter. She is produced as an embodiment of the fury of Hathor, and is her absolute antithesis. Where Hathor nurtures, Sekhmet destroys. Where Hathor is placid, Sekhmet is thirsty for blood. This blood is menstrual also, a symbol of independence, and a secretion of magickal import. Sekhmet's sly feline power epitomizes the guile accredited by the Egyptians to the forces of darkness, the flip side of the dignified holy chimera. Behind those watchful eyes may lurk the slippery quality of insidious evil.

Because of her fluidity and perfect attunement to the animal kingdoms, coupled with her higher intelligence, Sekhmet is a suitable shamanic totem. She can be approached as an aide to powers of insight, empathy, and camouflage. These qualities are of great use when astrally travelling, for example; particularly when one is on a particular mission. If under psychic attack, the art of disguise is invaluable, enabling one to travel to the source of the mischief, identify it, and hopefully stem it.

Sekhmet's alertness is another quality relevant to magickal endeavor. She never daydreams or misses a trick—watching a lioness with her cubs will confirm this; she combines the magickian's ideal traits of unflinching observation, grace, and power.

Lions being the majestic symbol of the sun, as well as kings (and queens) of the jungle, Sekhmet could be termed a solar warrior. Lion-heartedness is associated with generosity and an all-embracing nature (often with a soft center; see the *Wizard of Oz*), but Sekhmet, being female, is discriminating in her favor. She does not lack generosity, but is no pushover. Needless to say, she evinces the usual feline traits of arrogant courage coupled with cunning.

Traditionally, the solar domain is male-dominated and materialistic. It is the city of culture and commerce, as opposed to the arcady of lunar femininity. However, Sekhmet, being solar and feminine, combines the qualities of both camps, as, indeed, do several goddesses, being an enhanced projection of the human psyche; or the human psyche a diminished projection of original consciousness. She is a multifaceted deity who lends herself to a variety of functions, practical as well as magickal. For the purposes of this book, however, it is her shamanic aspect on which we will be focusing.

SHAMANIC ABILITY: PREPARATION

Shapeshifting is no mere fantasy; an adept can mimic the shape and form of any animal they choose (but the greater the fondness and knowledge of that form, the better); anything from a hornet to a horse. They are, however, usually detectable. The hornet, for example, is likely to be bigger and noisier than the ordinary insect, and shapeshifters often have a shimmering edge if you look properly. In the weirdest case scenario, the animal-form will bear the face of the person within. They are, after all, an astral chimera.

This may test the credibility level of some readers, who will perhaps hypothesize hypnotism or illusion as a possible source, but there are many who have witnessed such feats and, indeed, participated in them.

Admittedly, it can be an alarming experience at first, but fascination usually surpasses fear in such circumstances. This exercise, however, is designed to expand one's astral wardrobe and create an array of animal avatars, rather than to physically manifest animal-forms, though the line between the two is thin.

You do not need to take a special bath or shower prior to this visualization, but a pinch of incense on a charcoal disc will be helpful.

VISUALIZATION FOR SHAMANIC ABILITY

Sit cross-legged on the floor or bed, or lie supine if you can guarantee not to fall asleep. This position facilitates astral travel and vivid inner vision.

Imagine all of your seven major chakras spinning in unison, counterclockwise and then clockwise, with a propeller-like action. They whirr faster and faster, lifting your astral body away from the physical one and carrying it high into the air like a helicopter.

As it rises, try driving it. By concentrating on your crown and pineal chakras you can rise vertically into the air, while increased spinning of your lower chakras will even you out. Experiment for yourself, but don't forget to envision the correct color of each "propeller."

Now, imagine that the action of the chakras begin to produce a gossamer substance, a bit like protoplasm. Feel it cocoon and pulsate around you. This substance comes from you and is infinitely pliant to your own will. It will encase you in any form you choose—be it hawk, wolf, or serpent.

Decide on the animal you wish to become; attune your third eye to the third eye of a mental image of that animal. First be its mirror image, then *become* it.

Try shifting your shape through a variety of forms, and move (don't forget those chakras) accordingly. If you feel yourself fading or falling, take light from the ether and use that to sustain you.

As you *become* each animal, really try to think like it. Keep these thoughts basic and sensual—raw and elemental.

If you are an eagle, feel the spread of your wings, the breezes and winds that are your ley lines, your mastery of air, and your total belonging to this element. You might feel a keen hunger and find your vision piercing the hedgerows and fields far below for the movement of some tender morsel. You may just soar and swoop for the pleasure of it; feel the zephyrs in your feathers.

When you are wolf, smell the pine trees, the freshness of snow, and sense the hum of distant blood. Feel the network of your pack around you, your instinctive understanding of rhythm and vibration in the earth, of snort, glance, growl, and howl. Feel the heavy fur on your back; a pelt of camouflage as well as warmth. Feel the pad of your paws on the redolent earth. Run and test your muscle-power; feel the strength and health of your four limbs as they pound the ground, snapping twigs and scattering damp leaves and needles. Silently acknowledge the spirits of shelter and quarry; the only gods you know beneath the cold starry sky.

If you are a serpent, wriggle on your limbless belly; feel how all your power is concentrated into one thin line. No longer dissipated, your patterned flesh is potent and tactile to the single clause of your will. Hiss and rise up to strike an enemy, or exercise your authority with a warning. Feel your sibilant elasticity; the snaking S of your spine; the thick flakes of flesh packed around it. Attune yourself to reptile mythology; how misunderstood and maligned you are. Your python-self hooded the Buddha, after all, and you helped churn the lost amrita from the celestial Indian seas. What thanks do you get? None at all. It makes you spit.

For Sekhmet, the obvious choice is the lioness. To experiment successfully with this form you should concentrate on graceful alacrity, alertness, and majesty. Your unflinching poise reflects your pride and confidence. Nothing can perturb you, for all else is far, far beneath you. You are sleek with agile feline arrogance. Your teeth and powerful limbs ensure your rule is perpetuated. The atavistic traits of the infinitely superior cat family are made manifest in you, the beautiful and mighty one. You luxuriate with self-satisfaction until a movement in the grass provokes you to sudden fury. You kill the small animal without a second thought, punishing it for daring exist in your domain. The little dose of sweet blood tastes good. You will hunt some more if you get bored.

Do not forget to keep those chakras whirring and glowing. It is possible to envision them as working inside your animal body, covered by the relevant skin or pelt and, thus, invisible.

When you have finished experimenting, slow your chakras down and re-absorb the substance from which you created your animal-forms. If you like, you can keep them as they are and envision your aura as containing a compartment like a walk-in wardrobe. You may need to upgrade or rework parts of the animal-form the next time you put it on, but with any luck, most of its form will remain.

With constant practice, shapeshifting will become second nature, and you will be able, like all good shamans, to walk at will between worlds. The more frequently you masquerade in your animal-costume, the better it will fit. You will find new perceptions flooding your senses as you begin to exchange energies with the animal-genus concerned. This first-hand encounter with the animal kingdom certainly beats the more conventional methods of experiencing the diminishing world of Nature.

MUNDANE ARCHETYPES

The Sekhmet character is complex, clandestine, and infinitely variable. She experiments with personae as others do with clothes and hairstyles; she might have one for every occasion, a whole wardrobe of personalities, or limit herself to a few well-worn favorites. She is clever enough to slip into them with ease; her characteristic tactility ensures a superb fit, and she is equally at home in black, gray, or white.

Sekhmet is, of course, as fickle as she is adaptable, and her life will be characterized by experiments in sex, lifestyle, and religion. She is attracted to transsexuality and bisexuality, and gay men adore her. She is often found, indeed, encapsulated in a gay male body.

She is quick-witted, sleek, and catty, with excellent poise. She doesn't miss a trick. Intellectually adept and socially fluent, the Sekhmet character is capable of attaining great heights, particularly in the artistic and literary arena.

However, to those outside her circle of favor, she seems little more than a sly and sensual social courtesan, absorbed in the world of pride and artifice. She is prone to overindulgence, particularly in the name of art; the English artiste Stephen Tennant, living off pink champagne jelly in bed for twenty years, springs to mind.

To Sekhmet, the lure of conscious-altering drugs is considerable, especially opiates or those that are pleasure-inducing. Her willpower is strong enough to sustain her body through the extremes to which she relentlessly drives it in search of life's ultimate kick: she juggles with life and death and emerges laughing.

Sekhmet rarely adheres to a religious creed long enough for it to take effect, though she may be perversely attracted to Roman Catholicism or, more healthily, to Buddhism or Hindu-based creeds such as Krishnaism. She is most likely to be dismissive, having "tried and tested" a few, but will be partial to astrology, particularly tacky horoscopes, Tarot, tea leaves, and the crystal ball. She will be befriended by Hecate-types.

Despite this, she will often be as astrally spectacular as she is physically; and she is frequently flamboyant on this plane. If female, her strongest attachment will be to her children, for whom she would kill. If male, friends or possibly a partner will take precedence. She has strong intuition and powerful instinctive likes and dislikes, some of which may be xenophobic or classist. If you're in, you're in; if not, it's the big freeze.

Sekhmet is one of nature's starlets; a genuine adherent to "Do what thou wilt shall be the whole of the law." Some call her evil; others call her wonderful; but really, she is just a law unto herself.

TAROT CARDS

Strength, VII Cups, The World, The Fool.

GREEK GODDESSES

ARTEMIS

No man has ever touched this sacred flesh, molded by my will. Let no man ever touch it.

No will has ever dominated my will. Let no will ever taint it.

No hunter's bow has dispatched arrows with the surety of mine. Let none exceed me.

No cunning beast has ever outwitted my wit. Let none elude me.

No legs have ever outpaced my swift strong legs. Let none outpace me. No being has ever crossed me and survived. Let no one cross me.

No eye has ever scanned my virginity, and blinked again. Let all be blind who observe me.

For I am Zeus' daughter, protector of women and young girls, divine huntress and supreme Olympian athlete.

I am eternally young and rightfully proud.

None may displease me and expect to live.

Be warned, all who would sin against women and hold my daughters in contempt: you shall be hunted down like quarry and thrown to the dogs.

Be warned, all you women who ally yourselves with wrongful forces: even those of you who call yourselves my daughters. Treat your own kind with respect or you shall be doubly punished.

For I am Artemis Heccerge, who shoots from afar and never misses.

From me, though you may dodge behind trees and linger in tangled thicket, there is no hope of escape.

For the pursuit of the uncivilized is my sport and only pleasure.

THE NATURE OF ARTEMIS AND HER PRACTICAL APPLICATIONS

Artemis is the boyish girl of the Greek myths; often she displays more classically masculine traits than her brother Apollo. Indeed, though often regarded as a lunar deity, Artemis is rooted in logic and action. Her militant independence and uncompromising absorption in sporting activities create a female prototype unparalleled in other pantheons, and one with strong solar as well as lunar affiliations.

However, this spiritually potent dualism is irrelevant to Artemis unless it catalyzes and enhances action. Artemis is a goddess devoid of introspective capacity, choosing rather to mirror the animal world in which she runs free; a domain in which empathy between hunter and hunted would cause dysfunction. Artemis' selfishness is as essential to her as her bow, arrows, and hunting tunic.

Artemis defies both gender stereotypes and the expectations of society as a whole. Relentless in the pursuit of pleasure, the force of her will carries her above the group-mind that would categorize, integrate, and neutralize her. She operates alone, strong in her androgyny and eternal youth. Artemis' mental and spiritual growth has been arrested at adolescence; spiritually, one might even say at prepubescence. She is the tomboy teenager who never grows up.

Refusing to end the charmed and exhilarating adventures of childhood, Artemis is fiercely chaste, mercilessly slaying sexual transgressors and even those who glimpse her with her modesty compromised. As a warrior, she helps destroy the serpent Python and avenges the rapes of her protégée nymphs.

At play, she loves nothing more than running free in the woods with her swift strong pack, on the scent of some wild quarry. With her lean boy's body, narrow-hipped and minimally chested, her ability to flout the feelings and opinions of others with neither qualm nor guilt, and her pristine concentrated will, Artemis is the supreme athletic archetype. This lithe exemplar of holistic agility is an ideal role model for those with sporting aspirations, particularly serious ones. Athletics demands many of the traits Artemis so effortlessly exhibits—the ability to train relentlessly and the consequent foregoing of emotional preoccupations. There could be no better goddess to whom to appeal in matters physically competitive or demanding.

Artemis is a particularly appropriate totemic deity for women, especially those who prefer one another's company to that of men. She is a protectress of other boyish girls and has a strong distaste for the kind of flighty behavior engendered by Aphrodite. She is not adverse to heterosexual relationships per se, but when they occur, the participating woman must abandon her childhood memorabilia at Artemis' altar, consecrate her tunics to the maiden goddess, and leave the merry troupe of huntresses for good.

At childbirth, however, Artemis may appear again, her knowledge of instinctive matters aiding her ex-protégée through her tribulations. Bearing a flaming pine-torch symbolic of protective warmth, she welcomes the newborn infant into the world. Many women in ancient Greece prayed to Artemis as the celestial midwife. Mythologically, she is rumored to have helped deliver her own twin brother Apollo when their mother Leto was being harassed by the ever-jealous Hera. Perhaps this enmity helps explain Artemis' dislike of heterosexual interaction; her own mother's affair with a married god, Zeus, caused continual upheaval for all concerned.

Certainly, Artemis wants nothing to do with such silliness; her preoccupations are with dignity, strength, and sporting ability. She is also beautiful and proud of her looks; physical appearance is another of Artemis' domains. However, this self-nurturing goddess expresses nothing that is not primarily for her own pleasure. Narcissism and unwillingness to please others is the root of any vanity she and her priestesses harbor. Artemis will help you change *if you wish to do so of your own volition.* The criticisms of others, even those subconsciously stashed at the root of your motivation, will be disparaged and disregarded by Artemis, whose hauteur exists even vicariously. Be sure to analyze your reasons for conducting the visualizations for changing body shape. Neuroses will not impress this caustic, down-to-earth individual, so avoid petitioning her on their behalf.

APPROACHING ARTEMIS: PREPARATION

As Artemis is a maiden goddess, the new moon is the best time to access her. Like Hecate, she is a light-bearer, and the flaming torch is included in both goddess' symbolism: candles are, therefore, particularly relevant to her.

Cedar and pine oil, or a combination of moon and sun incense (both are widely available from New Age shops) will also be of benefit.

A cool, bracing shower will help—it is important to feel clean and capable prior to these meditations.

VISUALIZATION FOR CHANGING BODY SHAPE

For slimming purposes, concentrating on the throat-chakra will help you metabolize etheric energy through the medulla oblongata, lessening your desire and need for food. How useful this may prove, however, is another matter. Few magickal techniques can beat a healthy diet in conjunction with meditation and regular exercise. It was for these components, after all, that our bodies were designed.

The etheric body, which surrounds and merges with the physical body, contains the specifications for physical growth, as directed by the Higher Self and tailored by current thought processes and attitudes. The Higher Self may not have intended for us to have a stooped back, for example, but years of low self-esteem, shyness, or depression may have caused it to become so. Many illnesses, being almost without exception psychosomatic (even serious ones) begin in the etheric aura—thus, by keeping the aura clean, it is possible to dramatically reduce our chances of illness. Likewise, by manipulating the aura and maintaining the relevant mental attitude, the shape of the physical body may be altered, as it always follows where the etheric body leads. This is the principle behind the motto "think tall"; lofty attitudes really can increase one's height.

First, formulate your plan. Diet and exercise are the two most obvious ingredients for success. See the Magickal Diet and Exercise section at the beginning of the book for guidelines.

Now, stand before a full-length mirror by dim light. A low-watt bulb or candlelight are good, but natural dusk-light is perfect for magickal transformation processes.

You should be able to clearly see the parts of your body you are adjusting, so either work naked or scantily clad (a swimming costume perhaps); whichever feels best to you.

Burn a little sun and moon incense together, or evaporate some cedar or pine oil to help evoke the slender goddess Artemis.

Try to avoid mentally adopting the drifty, nebulous atmosphere that pervades at twilight. You will be employing its qualities to define your new body shape, but should remain mentally taut, like Artemis, and grounded in the physical.

Turn sideways, so that the mirror reflects your right shoulder, and take several slow, deep breaths. With each inhalation, charge yourself up with blue-white energy.

Contemplate the angular, boyish goddess with her fresh complexion, hunting tunic above the knees, and bow in hand. The straps of her quiver are slung across her chest, and inside this container you perceive a golden glow. Although Artemis' aura is often red (she received many blood sacrifices in arcane times in respect of her hunting aspect), when approached in her youngest form and as you concentrate on her youthful exhilaration while running through the pine forests, her exuberant liberty, she emits a silvery green glow. This is the Artemis whose help we wish to engender, so envision her as such.

Visualize a silvery green luminescence before you, slightly fir and pine-scented. Breathe it in and out until you feel attuned to it. From this miasma, witness the solid beginning to grow.

See Artemis' bearskin-shod feet, fleet as the wind, immaculately attuned to her mental command.

See her slender but strong legs, toned and honed to her will, capable of carrying her effortlessly, almost unconsciously, through forest, down vale, and over hill in the thrill of the chase.

Note the narrow hips girded with the chamois-colored hunting pelt; various throat-slitting tools at her waist. The golden arrows in the case emit a sunbeam-like radiance.

All of Artemis' features are streamlined for maximum speed: nothing is merely decorative; all is utilitarian.

See the arms, slim and strong, hued and burnished by the sun. The tendons are taut, poised to act in response to visual perception; but ease, the ease of confidence, permeates the celestial tomboy's stance.

Artemis' hair may be long, as envisioned by poets and artists throughout the ages, but she wears it as if short: modern Artemis has her hair cropped and defies impractical tresses.

The sky-blue eyes scan the air and earth in continual alertness; an inner intelligence interweaves the sounds and motions of realms both animal and human. Artemis moves effortlessly between the two, as fluent in instinct as she is in logic.

You may be aware of the hunting pack flanking the deity, but there is no need to visualize it unless you want to. Artemis rarely travels far without her loyal and well-groomed dogs.

Having breathed in her silver-green light, you are already connected to Artemis; strengthen the bond by taking one more deep breath of the wilderness goddess' light.

Feel your body, mind, and spirit being infiltrated by her untamed qualities of faultless instinct and independence; her childlike absorption in her own pursuits. Allow the silver-green light to permeate into and emanate from you. See yourself and Artemis coexisting inside this auric tent.

Now, turn to face the mirror, half-close your eyes and envision your body the way you would like it to be. Formulate your peripheral vision into the shape you aspire to attain. This is, as already mentioned, easiest done by dusk or candlelight, when you borrow shadows to help define the right proportions. Exaggerate the details in order to firmly impress them on your subconscious: you may even mentally caricature your future self.

Holding this etheric blueprint firmly in your mind's eye, ask for Artemis' help in attaining it. Imagine how good you will feel when you have it, and allow these positive feelings to flow into you now. As you continue to tailor your vision to your inner dictate, be aware of your body complying to it also.

Starting at the feet and moving up through ankles and calves, slowly flex your muscles and tendons and watch the two images merge. Where relevant, parallel your self-image to that of Artemis. Do not move until you can clearly see each part of your body conforming to your will. You are telling it what to do, giving it the new mold to which the atoms comprising your physical body will comply.

Continue this process right up to your head, and with the determination of Artemis, feel the energy of your new body, the confidence it will create, and know that this is your real future. Then embark upon the physical regime you have planned to help achieve it.

Repeat this exercise as often as possible, preferably once at morning, noon, and night. The more you surround yourself with this enthusiastically created body-mold, the sooner your body cells will comply to it.

You might also try walking around as if your body were already the way you want it to be. You are, after all, merely projecting yourself into your own not-too-distant future.

VISUALIZATION FOR SPORTING ABILITY AND FITNESS

As before, stand in a full-length mirror, either naked or in your swimming costume or sports clothes—whichever is most comfortable. Either way, make sure you can see all the muscles you wish to develop.

First, visualize clearly what you wish to achieve. If you are a pole-vaulter, see yourself gliding effortlessly over a high bar in a blaze of glory (hear people gasping and clapping if you so desire); if you are a gymnast, visualize yourself involved in feats of amazing stamina and suppleness. Most likely, you are just aiming for general fitness—in which case, envision your body exhibiting relevant qualities. Whatever your particular aim, the five stages of the following visualization will help you attain it.

THE FIVE Ss

The ingredients for success in the fitness and sporting arena are *suppleness*, *strength*, *speed*, *stamina*, and *surety*. The latter refers to accuracy in aiming—either yourself or your javelin, football, or discus. Cool confidence will help you attain a spot-on shot, hence the term surety.

Again, visualize your body the way you want it to be. Promise to yourself that you will become it. It does not hurt to exaggerate your visions to get your point across—for example, if you are looking for better muscle definition, you could imagine yourself absolutely bulging with muscles—it will impress your subconscious more if the image is striking and over-the-top.

Concentrate on Artemis until you feel her in the room with you. Feel the vigor emanating from her, her pitiless ambition, and her perfect will. Like her, you will let nothing come between you and your determination to succeed.

Watch yourself in the mirror, and begin to concentrate on suppleness.

Imagine that all of your limbs are snakes, infinitely tactile like the supreme reptile Python himself. Moving smoothly, emulate the serpent's silent slither. Enjoy the suppleness of your limbs for as long as it feels comfortable.

When you are ready, visualize the ultraconfident huntress' body of Artemis as your own, and stretch your limbs as if throwing a spear, drawing your bow, or stalking your prey. Like her, believe that you will never miss a shot. It is merely a matter of *how* perfect your feat of perfection will be.

Now, center on the faculty of strength.

At times of crisis, people have been known to perform feats of incredible strength; for example, women have lifted cars off of their hapless offspring. Clearly, extreme physical power is of a psycho-spiritual origin. The trick is not to require a disaster to precipitate it, but to have the confidence and determination available at all times, including, of course, when you are involved in your sporting events and activities.

Continue to stand in front of the mirror; now, imagine you are a bear. This animal is sacred to Artemis, and is a symbol of strength. Using the bear as a totem, you are going to imagine yourself holding the whole room up.

If possible, stand in a door frame to perform this part of the visualization; another option is to use weights so you can really feel the strain of your efforts. With feet planted apart at shoulder-width, hold the weights aloft or push against the top of the door frame as if you were supporting the roof of the room; as you do, concentrate on your incredible fortitude and bear-like brawn. Even if you are small, you can think big; as already mentioned, strength is not necessarily a function of the physical constitution. Imagine Artemis standing, holding high the body of a slaughtered monster in an exhibition of fortitude and prowess. The pain that you feel is an acknowledgement that your muscles are conforming to your mental image and will, so welcome it.

For stamina, continue this pose for as long as you feel apt. Make sure that when you desist you feel able to strike this pose again and again, ad infinitum, only you are not choosing to do so. It is good to push yourself to the limit, but not to the breaking point. Do not wait until you are weak with exertion, but quit while you are ahead. You are trying to impress upon your subconscious the fact that your strength knows no limits. Self-belief is half the composition of stamina.

Meanwhile, indefatigable Artemis is, of course, continuing in her tireless rounds of sporting activities. Stamina is not difficult to acquire when enthusiasm is combined with confidence.

For speed, imagine yourself streamlined like an arrow, being shot from Artemis' bow. Visualize yourself as a brilliant golden streak blessed with powers of incredible alacrity, outdistancing your competitors at the starting shot. As you watch yourself in the mirror, concentrate on how your limbs will lend themselves to the faculty of swiftness. You might also see yourself as Artemis involved in the chase; her only focus is the quarry; she is blissfully unaware of her body and simply honing in on the beast or monster concerned.

The final S is for surety.

Envision yourself as somebody who never misses the bull's-eye; somebody whose body is naturally drawn toward the goal. The goddess in this aspect was worshipped as *Artemis Heccerge*, meaning "the far shooter." From any distance, she can strike the goal. If you play football, *be* the football being kicked into the net. If you are a runner, *feel* the magnetic pull that draws your body through the finishing ribbon. You are like a bee making its way from flower to hive; a matter of instinct rather than navigation.

Consider the sharpness of your perceptions: your perfected ability to feel, hear, see, smell, taste, and instinctively attain the coveted goal. Most importantly, continue these exercises on a regular basis, preferably before you train. Refuse inwardly to acknowledge any adequacies; have total faith in your abilities. Of course, you must work on weak points, but they do not detract from your overriding competence.

Use Artemis, whose athletic abilities are unrivalled, as a totem and role model. Do not punish yourself for any difficulties you may encounter; nobody is born with the ability to vault sixty feet or run at sixty miles per hour. Mystics and yogis train in meditation and yoga for decades before they are able to wrestle tigers, lie on beds of nails, or levitate; but eventually they can. Know that with every visualization and every training session, you are drawing closer to your crowning success.

MUNDANE ARCHETYPES

Today's Artemis can be found in the Girl Scouts and similar same-sex institutions. At one time she confined her independent virginal nature to socially useful roles, but nowadays is given the leeway to express her more hedonistic side.

Artemis abounds in gay clubs and bars, is usually shorthaired, fresh-faced, and tomboyish, and is often attracted to those with identical interests and looks. She feels scorn for men and particularly for their sexuality, but in her newly liberated form is often forthright about her own sexuality within her own circle.

She has no time for ultrafeminine women, and would choose effeminate male company over theirs. She is inclined toward sports, computers, accounting, and management positions. Outside her own circle she is shy and gives every possible appearance of ordinariness.

The Artemis-type is secretly attracted to psychic studies and witchcraft, and may well have a pack of Tarot cards lying in her bottom drawer. Some of her sexual fantasies are orgiastic, but she is unlikely to live them out unless under the influence of a great deal of alcohol.

Although highly independent, she requires the support of friends, as she often feels that society is against her. She misses her "twin." She enjoys effete artistic men, but ultimately considers them pretentious. She has an acute sense of her own superiority, coupled with a disturbing conviction of sociological ineptitude.

Many Artemises refuse to acknowledge their sexuality and undergo one or two unsuccessful marriages before settling down with a dog or, occasionally, a cat. Artemis prefers monogamy, but may be forced to experiment in order to find a suitable partner. She makes an excellent mother, if given the chance to become or act as one, and is aware of all aspects of her children's needs. However, she in no way requires this role to embellish her sense of self. She is used to solitude.

Career-wise, the Artemis archetype will go far, against the odds. Hard work and acquired skill combined with her iron will make her a workforce to be reckoned with.

TAROT CARDS
The Moon, The Star, III Cups.

PERSEPHONE

Pale hands and long fingers; artistic, my mother used to say. Supple as a willow, with that pearlescent hue.

Even then, I was silver instead of gold. It seems there is no escaping the Fates.

I liked to spin a tale or two myself: singing, mirrored, and by moonlight I wove my dreams and symbols into mats and cloths and placed them in my mother's halls. Flora and Proserpina. My two personae.

I already knew, you see.

Mad girl, some said, but I'd had a presentiment of Pluto. I used my long pale palms to shake the bones, and from these bones I divined my capture. A noose of black hair fell across my right eye and snaked about my throat.

Nothing can be done, my friend the Oracle smiled. Your future belongs to your past, Persephone. She had an annoying habit of speaking in oxymorons; she thought it made her sound more convincing. Her tutor the sphinx taught it to her.

Hecate stood by with her pack of dogstars, nodding as if everything we said she knew already; it was only natural. She looked very mysterious, though, when I probed her further.

It will be, she said.

I could've screamed.

It was Hecate the torchbearer who told my mother of my whereabouts after the abduction. She spied him out, the wily crone that she is; it is possible that she knew in advance. I prefer to think otherwise; I do not want to accuse her of letting me be raped.

I wish that she, or anybody living, were here now.

My loneliness echoes through the chambers of Hades; my husband hears it and is affronted. Even as a child bride crowned Queen of the Underworld he felt my duress as a strain on his heart, and turned an accusatory eye on me. He wields a stinging whip of guilt; down here, it is easy to forget where the truth lies.

I should, he says, be soft and pliant like the flower-gatherer he originally knew. I dare not tell him that no stalagmite, no ancient moss or dripping lichen can console me for the loss of my mother's feats of fragrant grace: narcissi, hibiscus blossoms—words like spells of bright spring flowers cast upon the rich green earth. He cannot make me happy with his solemn declarations of love, nor with his gloom-embued love-tokens and gifts of baleful power; but I have learned to watch.

I watch the souls of the newly-dead arrive by boat; anxious captives awaiting their fate. I give them orders and, as I do, I try to gain some sense of what is going on above. Sometimes, if they died outside, I can smell the sunlight in their spirit-hair. With these, for old time's sake, I share a drink.

The dead brew a bitter draft in the recesses of my husband's domain. It tastes of wormwood and regret; temporarily, it helps us forget our present and, like giddy revenants on the midnight staircase, revisit our past. I used to use it all the time, until I found that it was nibbling nasty little holes into my soul. Now I touch seldom a drop. I have become quite ascetic in my tastes. Possibly, I have been down here for too long.

I await my release with patience, however. I have established a dim subterranean order in my life, and now the upper world seems a chaos of color and noise. Even my mother's corn-colored hair, once my delight to stroke and plait, seems a brazen blaze to my dilated vision. I have learned a thousand shades of gray, the differing textures of shadows.

My spirit-forms will miss me when I go, but I know my due. I will sup at a more wholesome cup; I will get my share of sunlight in my hair.

But always, always, no matter where I am, I must return. My present is always my past, and my past my future.

Such is the rotation of the Wheel of Life.

THE NATURE OF PERSEPHONE AND HER PRACTICAL APPLICATIONS

Persephone's myth is perhaps best known as an allegory of seasonal change. It is also one of the most popular stories bequeathed to us by the ancient Greeks, providing a vivid portrayal of archetypal energy patterns and personalities. It is summarized here, as to approach Persephone without an understanding of her history would be futile.

As a child, Persephone lived in her mother Demeter's domain among the fruitful fields and groves of Mount Olympus. She was known as *Kore*, meaning maiden, and was surpassingly beautiful. Demeter sent her to earth to protect her from the lustful advances of the other gods; some accounts claim that she went to Sicily.

Pluto, dark god of Hades, was among her admirers. He asked for her hand in marriage, but sunny Demeter was aghast at the idea of Kore steeped in the shadows of the dead, and refused.

So one day, when she was out gathering flowers, Pluto snatched her away to the Underworld and forced her to become his Queen.

Demeter, deeply distressed by the abduction of her daughter, wandered the earth in desolation, until she came to rest in queen Metaneira's palace in Eleusis. In disguise and still befuddled by grief, she became the baby prince's nursemaid until, surprised in an attempt to confer immortality on him by placing him in the fire, she angrily revealed her true identity to the horrified Metaneira.

From then on, Demeter's mourning reached new depths, and she withdrew the faculty of fecundity that had kept the soils rich and the leaves green on the trees, causing an instant interminable winter. With the nature goddess refusing to give her bounty, it looked as if all might starve unless the earth mother was consoled by her daughter's safe return.

Eventually, with Hermes and Iris as intercessors, a compromise was reached. Persephone, who had eaten of a cursed pomegranate while in Hades and, consequently, could not leave it permanently, would be returned to earth for six months, but abide in Hades for the other six. This would restore Demeter to her rightful state of beneficence long enough for humans to stock up to tide themselves over the barren months.

So, during spring and summer, Persephone walks with her mother and enjoys release from the weighty solemnity of the Underworld. During late autumn and winter, however, she is duty-bound to preside over the realms of the dead, whose secrets she knows and whose welfare is her responsibility.

Persephone's story has an Eden-like quality. Her early life is idyllic, spent in innocent enjoyment and living in the light; but when her sexuality becomes pronounced, she is instantly transferred to the dark realms of fear and confusion. She is snatched from grace by a desire over which she has no control; consequently, one of the psychological features she represents is that of strong subconscious urges, especially those with drastic repercussions.

On one level, Persephone has become trapped in the realization of her body: she has fallen from the high vibration of innocence into the low, slow vibration of material enslavement. The Underworld represents the entrapment of the physical plane; the godless realms of drudgery and negative thought that often mark our transition into adulthood, or reality. Demeter's domain is symbolic of the original god-informed state, metaphorically the *Satya Yuga* or Atlantean Age, when thoughts were elevated and physicality barely relevant. This is the tale of innocence and experience of the Greek myths; there can be little doubt that Persephone gains in wisdom what she loses in liberty.

Persephone's descent into the Underworld is the psychic and psychological initiation referred to in the Eleusinian Mysteries. She raises herself from victim to psychopomp, from hapless child to wise and tacit priestess, becoming her own source of light in the profound darkness of the Underworld. Ultimately, she becomes conversant in both realms, with power within each. This is a suitable allegory for the level we inhabit, comprised of contrasts and duality—a realm in which, unless we know darkness, we cannot truly appreciate light, and where pleasure is redoubled by the previous experience of and release from pain.

Persephone's demi-release from Hades also represents her ability, gleaned in the occult gloom of the Underworld, to release herself at least partially from the bondage of materialism and the flesh. The magic she learns in Hades is that of transcendence—she realizes that goodness comes from a source independent of external stimuli and physical manifestations.

Thus her story also symbolizes the process of self-realization; a nose-dive into the murkiest aspects of the psyche; the inner treasure salvaged and brought to the surface. The Hades experience is much akin to "crossing the abyss" in magickal terms: facing and transcending one's fears and phantoms. Though we have fallen from grace—Eden, the Satya Yuga, the Atlantean Era, or whatever one wishes to call it— we are not entirely bound. By processes of solitude, magick, and meditation (mantric is purported to be the most effective form of yoga in this era) we can, like Persephone, transcend back into the light and liberation of the original soul-state. Even the most unenlightened being escapes to the soul-refuge and recharge point in dreamless sleep and between incarnations. How much more powerful, then, to bring it through to the conscious realms.

Consequently, Persephone's gifts are those of sublimating depression into epiphany and rebirth, and the wisdom thus engendered. One undergoes the trials and tribulations of the Underworld, receives knowledge beyond that which is available in more pleasant surrounds, and finally ascends—but only for a while. Persephone (and her initiate) must accept the cycles that will inevitably change her circumstance, for better or for worse, and not allow the shadow of Hades to hang over and inhibit her while she is above ground. Likewise, she must concentrate on her duties as Queen of the Dead when she is in that role: daydreaming about picking flowers would be detrimental if she neglected her subterranean tasks. This, of course, demands a particularly philosophical overview—an acceptance of her lot in its entirety. Only in this way can Persephone find peace of mind.

Similarly, we must accept our fate and work within rather than against it. This encompasses the factors that are unchangeable; the features of our lives that, maybe for the sake of others, or perhaps through practical impossibility, we cannot alter.

Persephone also indicates the need for balance, a knowledge of both outer and inner realms.

Worldly sophistication is nothing if not balanced by spirituality and the capacity of renunciation; likewise, in order to live successfully in both domains, it is necessary to abide in society and understand to some extent the minds of others.

Many ascetics provide services of incalculable value to mankind, from a solitary Himalayan cave or temple temenos; however, this yogic strain and capacity is rarely (if ever) found in the West. Occidental reality dictates that a foot in both worlds is the most balanced and progressive route to liberation. This is the equipoise that Persephone perfectly exhibits.

OVERCOMING REGRET AND DEPRESSION: PREPARATION

The Persephone archetype is of particular relevance to those who feel their mood swings and depressive urges are beyond their control, and whose minds are bending under the conviction that they are "going mad." Symptoms particular to this deity include symbolic dreams, presentiments and attention to omens or auguries; menstrual highs and lows; and tendencies toward Gothic imagery, thought processes, and even music. For those who feel that their objective circumstances are the root cause of their despond and who are looking for a lighter form of self-healing, Sarasvati is recommended in lieu of Persephone.

In Persephone, outer circumstances provide a metaphor for internal reality. The negative aspects of one's life: ill-health, arguments, or charmless surrounds, reflect the inner reality: grief, regret, or depression. Likewise, positive or neutral traits are paralleled on the physical plane. Her mindset is the key to self-transformation, and it is with this knowledge that we approach Persephone, the astral analogue of our own condition.

Although the most pernicious form of regret is self-blame, there are many shades in Hades, and several are "what if" and "if only" thoughts. We can drive ourselves to distraction with conjecture and the "grass is always greener" conviction that our alternative life-route would have been more rewarding, loving, prestigious, and so on; especially if our personal choices have led to tragedy. This may take any form; it is our own interpretation of the situation that makes it so. Consequently, one is left feeling bereft, often too intimidated by more potential suffering to make further life-decisions. How can this paralysis be cured? Persephone can help remedy it by raising the consciousness above the ephemeral and helping us to see that all probability levels contained this same lesson, in one form or another. The process, however painful, was necessary for individual soul-development; and, more fatalistically, this is the life we were "meant" to lead.

These and lateral thought processes are a suitable preamble to the Persephone visualizations; but they are not to be perceived as excuses. Meditation on the Higher Self and its all-pervasive influence on our lives, however obfuscated by trivia and disbelief, will be highly beneficial prior to approaching Persephone.

A ritual bath is not necessary; nor is internal calmness and serenity. Persephone is best approached when one is feeling intense.

Lunar herbs such as rosemary and mint may be helpful in evoking this goddess' presence in your psyche.

Basically, however, all you require is your confusion, misery, and imagination.

VISUALIZATION FOR OVERCOMING REGRET AND DEPRESSION

Take a few deep breaths, and think of the experience you wish to transform as existing in the Underworld.

Envision it literally underground, and yourself inside it; in a dark labyrinthine prison if the problem is complicated; in a simple but scary maze if it is less so. Fill it with the symbols of your circumstance—for example, people whose input influenced the situation might be represented by masks or pictures on the wall, and you might be wearing something indicative of your state of being when the crisis hit.

Walk around your previous life. Try to feel the same emotions, desires, and concerns you had then, and to think the same thoughts. If you have always felt this way, then imagine your present circumstances as existing underground, surrounded by the symbolic paraphernalia relevant to your depression.

If this process causes you pain, imagine the pain as arrows shot into you as if you were quarry; pluck them out and keep them in a bundle in your hand.

If you can, it is good to physically enact plucking out the arrows. Either way, make sure you have them all.

Now, recall the moment the crisis hit. If there is no specific time, pick a happy memory and focus on that instead. Then, remember how you found yourself plummeting into the chthonic chaos of the Underworld; grappling for a hold but finding none; falling lost through inner space. You had been caught in a net; a trap. For a moment all points of reference were lost—there was just the sensation of accelerating descent. Then, with a shuddering crash, you landed in the scene of your present circumstances—in the Underworld.

Here you are, still caught in the trap.

Look down at your body still swathed in the netting. To get anywhere, you are first going to have to break through this spider's web of misfortune.

Cut or tear yourself out of the net. Remember, this net represents the circumstances that brought you here, and its strength and consistency will reflect this.

Take as long as you need to get out of the net.

When you do, bundle it up and keep it with the arrows.

Now, sit up and look around. You feel lonely and afraid; the shadows flicker like dark flames on the tall walls around you; your movements echo eerily in the cavernous chambers.

Spend a couple of moments really feeling your vulnerability and fear; you clutch your net and arrows and look around for something or some-one to help you. You feel like a child who is without its mother for the first time. Everything looks big and full of potential danger. You long for some protection or comfort, but your only source is far, far away. The icons in your chamber are mute, immobile. Your gaze flicks frantically across the walls and corridors of glowering darkness, seeking some relief.

As it does, you notice an eerie light coming from your left. The sil-very luminescence gradually brightens the scene; in fact, isn't that a path at your feet?

Looking closer, still holding the net and arrows as if they were a talis-man, you see that you are standing on a black and white tiled and wind-ing pavement that feels vibrant through the soles of your feet. You get the impression that it might lead somewhere interesting. You have little to lose—there is nothing for you here now—so you decide to trace the palely illuminated path to its source.

As you walk, you move deeper into the heart of Hades.

The air smells musty and heavily recycled, and sits like a dusty blan-ket on your chest. You begin to long for something fresher and more wholesome. You quicken your pace.

Soon there is nothing left to see but the bleak barren slopes of the imprisoning walls and the black and white checkered tiles of the marble floor. You are a solitary chess piece in an abandoned game. This place is forsaken of the gods, an area few consciousnesses would choose to visit. You begin to wish you had stayed in the little corner of Hades which you knew—at least it held symbols you recognized, and reminded you of home.

With one fingertip you nervously caress an arrow-point, barely aware of your body. You are watching the path become a wider floor, suggestive of some kind of portal.

It takes you just a few more steps to reach a black pillar to the left and a white to the right. Between them, the light is strong. You continue to move toward it.

At the center of the refulgence is revealed the figure of a cloaked and veiled woman. She sits upon an impressive stone throne, elaborately carved with figures of mythological beasts, three-headed dogs, and crowds awaiting passage across the treacherous river Styx. Skulls adorn the armrests. The woman's skin is very white, so white that it glows in the dark, as do her incongruously sky-blue eyes. The veil is thin and her visage shines dimly behind it. The long tresses that frame the thin but pleasing face are so black they look as if they have been cut out of the air to reveal the void behind light. Her garments are white and blue; rather drab. Her thin lips are smiling slightly, but she says not a word. She looks at you in tacit nonchalance, though she is not unkind. In her hands she holds a voluminous rolled-up scroll of thick vellum. You get a tantalizing glimpse of the mysterious script that embellishes it, but nothing more.

Not wishing to be intrusive or appear rude, you realize that you must introduce yourself to the luminous goddess you now realize is Persephone, and present your case to her possible grace.

You kneel before her, place your bundle on the floor in front of you, raise your hands prayer-style, and request her help. Explain that you have accidentally fallen into the Underworld from above; that you do not feel it is your time to be here, but that something keeps dragging you down. This began after the particular crisis (describe it if you wish); you would very much appreciate Persephone's help in restoring you to your pre-incident peace of mind.

The Queen of the Dead nods awhile, half indicative of comprehension, half of empathy. Recognition of your circumstance registers on her face, which is beginning to show compassion now.

You realize that she is thinking that she too would like to return above ground, but that she cannot. Her bright blue eyes convey an acute telepathy the likes of which you have never encountered before. Before you know it, you the supplicant and Persephone the deity are involved in a silent conversation.

You explain to her that you have learned a great deal from your fall and the time you have spent in the Underworld, but that you would like to return to the realms of the living in order to express your new-found life-skills.

It is essential to invest this statement with belief and enthusiasm. The greater your conviction, the more likely Persephone is to help you.

The problem is, of course, that you still feel encumbered by the emotions and situations engendered by the circumstance that propelled you down here in the first place. You gaze hopelessly at your arrows and net.

Persephone follows your gaze and smiles. Still without a word, she unrolls the vellum and hands you a quill. You instinctively understand that you are to write down your feelings and hurts, the things that are holding back your progress; you are to perform a thorough catharsis that Persephone will then guard for you, along with the bundles of arrows and net.

Now, *really* let yourself go with this. If possible, physically write things down as you envision your writing material being Persephone's vellum and quill. Be as honest and purgative as you possibly can. Let it all out. Spend as long as you need in this process.

When you have finished, Persephone smiles and rolls the scroll up tight again. If you have physically committed your angst to paper, roll that up too. You will not look at it again. At the end of the exercise you will burn or bury it.

Persephone also takes the arrows and net into her safekeeping. She is effectively removing the causes of pain that have led you to this untimely descent into the Underworld.

She hands you a burning torch. As you thank her, be aware of the wisdom you have accrued during your time in Hades and in her divine presence. This is the only thank-you Persephone really requires.

Persephone inclines her head and you instantly ascend.

With the torch lighting your Persephone-propelled way, you arrive at the same scene from which you began your journey, only now it is imbued with fresh air and light. See your friends and family walking about here, looking animated and brighter than the gloomy masks you envisioned before. Feel yourself in your new role as light-bearer where previously you were the raven of doom.

You know that if you fall again, you will be able to enlist the goddess' help once more, and that your appreciation of the world of the living will be all the stronger for having been denied it a while.

Breathe the luminescence of your new lease of life and fill your lungs with the bright prana of pleasure and potential. Keep inhaling and exhaling this light until your whole body is as aglow with golden refulgence as Persephone's was with silver energy.

When you are embued with solar light in every pore, a positive sun deity yourself, it is time to open your eyes.

MUNDANE ARCHETYPES

The mundane Persephone archetype exists almost exclusively as a teenager. She is quiet, intelligent, and artistic; she enjoys French symbolist poets, Gothic imagery, and surreal and symbolist art. She is always seeking outward expressions of her inner turmoil, and her own creative work is highly metaphorical.

She is both vulnerable to and suspicious of men, her instinctual urges posing a serious threat to her intellectual decisions. Her faculty for self-control is self-denial. She is prone to fainting, visionary experiences, and psychism.

The Persephone archetype has strong religious proclivities, which are likely to vent themselves through unorthodox channels such as occult interests. She may be drawn to Wicca and, indeed, formulating a personal relationship with the earth and earth mother will be highly beneficial to her; however, she will eventually find this outlet intellectually unsatisfying. Instead she may turn to High Magick, in which she will prove highly proficient, but she will be easy prey to the manipulative egos that haunt that field of endeavor. She is generally better working alone or with friends.

She is likely to reject her mother (who has, she feels, abandoned her), while inwardly, perhaps only semiconsciously, craving the comfort and nurturing she represents. Instead, she will form obsessive spiritual feelings toward another, possibly of the same sex, and when those feelings spill over into physicality, she will face much confusion. Her high ideals do not correlate with the laws of the material world.

Only inner development and the company of similar empathetic beings (women and androgynous males) will ease the neuroses and perpetual loneliness felt by this typical misfit teenager. Eventually, with the aid of good therapeutic friendships and self-expression, she will develop into another archetype—ideally, of the Demeter or Empress nature. She will travel through shades of Hecate, Sekhmet, Isis, and many others en route.

In the meantime, she will suffer from taking herself too seriously and from being misunderstood by the emotionally less intelligent and spiritually less developed people who inevitably surround her.

TAROT CARDS
The High Priestess, The Moon.

HECATE

It has been a prosperous month for Corinna and her husband. Their olive groves have flourished in the clement weather and Corinna's stomach is swelling like a fruit with another ripening child. Their two sons and daughter are growing up strong and bright. As the moon has reached her fullness, so too have their fortunes waxed.

Carefully she prepares her gifts of bread, wine, wild bee's honey, and corn cakes. Into each she invests a portion of herself: a thank-you to the goddess of bad fortune for keeping away; a request for a healthy pregnancy and easy birth when the time is right. The midwife who roots among the herbs at night knows how to deliver a blessed child.

In her cocoon of light she makes ready these offerings, the unnerving feeling of being watched only slightly counteracted by the warmth of the oven

HECATE

•

158

When her preparations are complete, Corinna ensures that the children are safe in their beds and leaves the villa to her husband's watchful eye.

She takes her gifts, wrapped in fresh white linen, spun by her own hand at the dark of the moon, lights a torch, and leashes one of the dogs from the yard. She is methodical in her actions, attempting with practical concerns to eradicate a little of the sensation of a set of beady eyes on her, but Hecate is strong tonight—stronger than Corinna's sanity. Strange thoughts rise unbidden in her mind, as they always do when she makes this journey. Moods infest her blood and storm the flimsy barricades of reason; she dwells on what might have been, on the soul of her unborn child, on the memories of childhood, of other lives.

Barefoot, she makes her way toward the crossroads, one league away. A chill breeze makes the hair on her arms rise; she wraps her thin shawl closer to her skin.

Except for the light thud of her feet on the deserted path, her breathing and the dog's eager panting, all is quiet. No noise disturbs the silence of the pines, their bristling darkness flanking her on both sides. Animals hold their breath as the firelit woman and her dog make their winding pilgrimage through the dark woods.

Eventually, Corinna reaches the crossroads.

A triple-headed stake marks the place, fashioned with the body of a snake from which a mare, dog, and lion glare.

Silently, she kneels and calls to Hecate.

She leaves her sacrifice.

As she hears the woman's footsteps receding, a luridly painted child emerges from the bushes.

Her rumbling stomach reminds her of her real mission here. She gathers the foodstuffs, and those left by Hecate's other pilgrims, with grateful haste. She will share it with some of the others. She has not tasted good wine for a month now—though she often smells it on men's breath—this offertory flagon will be a special treat.

Hooknosed Hecate watches from the tree.

The next time she sees Corinna, it will be in the presence of the blood of life.

THE NATURE OF HECATE AND HER PRACTICAL APPLICATIONS

Hecate is variously described as a crone, a three-faced lunar goddess, and a seductive priestess of the occult. Her indubitable skills as a sorceress make her capable of being any or all of the above; indeed, she inhabits the body best suited to the aspect she is currently displaying. In autumn she is likely to manifest as a wily old lady wrapped in a billowing cloak; during festivals or sabbats she may choose to appear in her symbolic three-headed form. To those excited by the power she represents, maybe a little glamoured by it, she will seem mesmerizingly, perhaps overtly sexual.

Whatever her appearance or phase, Hecate is intimately associated with the moon, and is mistress of the night. She is said to ride the dark night skies in her lunar chariot, her star-fire torch burning with an icy, supernatural light, confirming her mastery of land, sea, air, and fire. Her three faces represent the three major stages of the lunar cycle: new, full, and dark, and it is with the latter that she is particularly associated. These stages have long been paralleled with feminine development, their correspondences being maiden, mother, and crone, respectively. Consequently, she also presides over the menstrual cycle, whose synchronicity with the lunar month has always been recognized as significant.

The essence of this deity is as untenable as moonlight; she often manifests as intuition, dreams, and symbolic experiences. One translation of her name is "She who works from afar." It is said that only dogs can sense Hecate's whereabouts; they were sacred to her and used as sacrificial offerings. Dogmeat was eaten in her honor. She is the supreme witch, without whose presence no coven is complete.

One of the most important aspects of magickal training is challenging the neophyte's beliefs and, particularly, her prejudices. Within witchcraft, the domain in which Hecate is queen, a deliberate attempt is made to reclaim taboo areas of the psyche and, indeed, to revel in them as a counterreaction to their previous suppression. This includes three of the most powerful forces in our lives: social (inbred) mores, sex, and death. The witch's sabbat was for many centuries an orgiastic, atavistic replay of fertility rites, Pan worship, and saturnalia, only heightened by church-inspired neuroses. The idea was not just to revive the pagan gods, but to regain conscious control of the primal faculties and harness their profound effects on our lives. These goals remain today, though the mode of attaining them may have changed somewhat.

The artist and occultist Austin Osman Spare perhaps epitomized this aspect of the occult and Hecate's place in it (from his personal standpoint) through his relationship with his patron, Mrs. Paterson, and the rituals, sigils, and drawings that ensued. His obsession with the crone and her hideous, beguiling sexuality took the concept of being hagridden to a suitably challenging and liberal degree.

The chaotic, seemingly negative side of our psyches has its place. Hecate, as patroness of prostitutes, thieves, and beggars, not to mention witches, protects those on the outskirts of society. She spreads her volumous cloak around the feared and hated, the outcast and "inferior." She represents the objective eye searing through the elaborate facade of standard society. She is the original socialist. Riches and education cannot deceive her; she views the heart. When the heart is a little nibbled by the worms of misfortune, she proffers a healing vial.

Hecate does not judge, except on respect extended in her direction. To those who do not have the emotional intelligence necessary to encompass her, she will seem the most terrifying of harridans.

Being the crone, Hecate embodies the repulsion felt particularly in the West for physical frailty and the subsequent threat of death. Occidental society is becoming one in which plastic surgery is touted as the necessary alternative to the visible experience of the life-adept, otherwise known as wrinkles and crow's feet; a hierarchy in which the tradition of tribal ancients is so overruled by youth culture that the old do indeed seem to have become empty vessels. If one is perceived as nothing, it is very difficult to maintain a sense of something. For the marginalized agèd, Hecate could prove a feisty antiboredom serum and a powerful elixir of lust for life, which often manifests as active intelligence.

This archetypal witch, vaunter of the unpalatable, can make or break masks at will. She is generous in offering third chances when others stall at a second.

Hecate is the bearded woman, champion of untouchables, bringer of menstrual madness. No hormone replacement can shake this devil from our back, for she is the part of us that is perennially unacceptable. She is the counterreaction to all insecurities; the part of the psyche that rebels against feeling outcast. The cause could be anything from the physical (too fat, too bald, the "wrong" race), to bi- or homosexuality, to the harboring of unpopular convictions (for example, paganism in a Catholic school), to the age-old inferiority complex. Hecate is willing to help any who are outcast.

Traditionally, Hecate is the guardian of the crossroads, particularly those involving the conjunction of three roads. Because of her unique relationship with and position of supremacy in the system of maiden-mother-crone (usually construed as Artemis-Demeter-Hecate, or Selene-Aphrodite-Hecate), she rules over feminine functions including, of course, childbirth and menopause. Her sacred numbers are three and nine in respect of this triple goddess aspect.

As well as a crafty midwife to gods and mortals, Hecate is a succoring shadow at death. She was the only person to witness Persephone's abduction and subsequent rape in the Underworld, and helped Demeter trace her hapless daughter. When it was established that Persephone had eaten part of a pomegranate and thus could not be fully released from Hades, Hecate became her part-time companion in the subterranean gloom.

Hecate may be a hag and protector of outcasts, but her reign is supreme in her own domain. In her, we find all the wisdom and capability that shamanic cultures attribute to age; a sublime transcendence of worldly concerns. She has surpassed youth and its cravings for family, partnership, and prestige, moved beyond the disillusionment process that often accompanies middle age, shed all concern for what others think of her, and settled into the habitual trusting of her own judgment. She does not discriminate between those in a fortunate life-cycle and those whose karma holds them at the bottom of the wheel of fortune. As guardian of the latter, she renders sacred the profane and befriends the pariah. Consequently, the Hecate godform can help lance the fear behind prejudice, often disguised behind a curtain of sanctimony, and bring cosmic balance into situations of discrimination. She is the Justice of the Darkside.

As well as acting as an equalizer, the presence of Hecate enlivens powerful magickal currents and declares the omnipotence of the soul. A variety of personae, magickal and psychological, become available to us when Hecate is near. Past incarnations, or nomadic archetypal personalities, come to the fore for the purposes of exploration. Psychism becomes pronounced. Inner development and increased occult awareness are inevitable in Hecate's presence, but the road may not be easy. Hecate, being the dark and wily aspect of the triad, is unlikely to pick for us the simplest route at the crossroads, but rather the one that will challenge us to the fullness of our capacity. Mediumistic and wise she certainly is, but she'll give you a run for your money.

The flipside of Hecate's gift of profound wisdom is the threat of egoism. Hecate may be the Queen of the Witches, but all too often one finds her mundane archetypes making the same claim. Hecate's powers are available to all, and are not confined to one person or group of people. Traits vary in strength, but Hecate herself would be the first to agree that all godforms are different, but equal; that all beings, great or small, are equally God. The difference is only in the manifestation.

ENCOUNTERING HECATE

If you are female, it is easiest to access Hecate either during your period or just before it. If you have PMS, all the better; your hag-aspect can be used to your advantage.

Autumnal influences will be of benefit, as will working with the dark-side of the moon.

The best time to contact Hecate is any major sabbat (see glossary), particularly Samhain (October 31st) or the Winter Equinox. However, all godforms are available at all times if a suitable mental environment is created for them to inhabit. In Hecate's case, a strong awareness of the seasons as reflected in nature will help.

Concentrate on this hooknosed crone, dressed in her black cloak and cackling alarmingly, one eye seeming to pierce your soul from out of her lopsided, cowled face. She may be bent and crooked, but she demands respect, and you instinctively give it.

She is surrounded by her colors: purple, mauve, and black. Candles of these shades of darkness will help evoke the goddess.

There are some good Hecate incenses (and recipes) available if you are looking to create a ritualistic atmosphere to enhance your visualization and spellworking.

A walk in the local park, during the day if it is autumn or winter, or at twilight or night if it is summer or spring (needless to say, be cautious), is another suitable preamble to channeling Hecate. Pay attention to the trees, flora, and fauna, and feel the life-currents flowing through the elements, manifesting in people and patterns of humanity everywhere. Feel the mystery behind it; the power of the cosmic intelligence that directs all growth and decline. Hecate lives in the magic behind the veil, and her presence gives depth to shadows, highlights the luster of red and green leaves, bestows life with a tingle of anticipation, and causes candlelight to become entrancing; a flaming torch leading us to new astral worlds.

OVERCOMING PREJUDICE: PREPARATION

For Hecate, it seems particularly apt that readers should create their own visualization. However, as it can be difficult to work without structure, I have provided the skeleton by using a personal example presented in the first person. Readers are then free to adjust the details to suit themselves.

Most of us undergo, from time to time, the infinitely distressing experience of being discriminated against. The sensation of being "ganged up on" can reinvoke the worst aspects of childhood, undermining confidence and making it difficult to maintain an adult personality. Frustration, anger, and hurt can be a debilitating combination; a fact of which, of course, our assailants are well aware. Work situations, in which colleagues are both bored and looking to elevate themselves in the eyes of their peers, often provide the right environment for a spite-attack.

VISUALIZATION FOR OVERCOMING PREJUDICE

A few years ago I was obliged, in impecunious circumstances, to take a part-time job in a clothes shop. Unfortunately, I was instantly ostracized for my "studenty" looks and accent, and treated brusquely or ignored—except to be looked up and down and whispered about.

In some respects, I found it an interesting lesson in anthropology, but there were times when I dreaded going into work for another day of being cold-shouldered and criticized. Despite my perpetual friendliness, every effort was made to make me feel bad. It began to work.

I started at the clothes shop in April, and by Beltane (May 1st), I'd had just about as much as I could take. I wanted to keep the job; it was easy and I needed the money, but I was seriously considering packing it in simply to evade the psychological torment it involved.

Right from the beginning I used self-protection techniques without which I would surely have quit in the first week, including the effective method of visualizing myself with a flaming violet aura (sometimes yellow or orange to avoid being too standoffish: purples can be rather intense and serious). However, at Beltane I was inspired to use a more dramatic technique—that of bending the minds of my colleagues to an angle from which my idiosyncrasies would seem interesting rather than alienating. I also wanted them to shed any insecurities or prejudices (as far as possible) that were causing this reaction in the first place. A tall order, one might think, but as I discovered, all I had to do was concentrate my will and ask.

The first thing I did was walk in the park until I felt attuned, as mentioned in the preparations section. Amazingly, the park nearest to me at the time had a statue of Hecate at its gate (in Victorian times it had been a botanical garden of some standing, and the four seasons were represented as statues at the entrance); this was an obvious pilgrimage point, and helped me align myself with the goddess. I also concentrated on the crone and her symbols and colors, and imagined her walking through the park, scattering autumn leaves on the breeze as she passed.

For the visualization, I used a small black candle to represent the resistance of the women and the negativity they felt toward me, and a silver pentacle, which stood for my beliefs, idiosyncrasies, and essence. I placed the candle on top of the pentacle. Then I strongly visualized each of my colleagues in turn and mentally transferred their feelings of antipathy into the candle. Once I felt the candle was imbued with every ounce of negativity they felt for me, I asked for Hecate's aid and lit it. As the candle burned, I envisioned their resistance, fear, and hostility being burned away. I did this for five minutes on three consecutive days at the same time; I started at Beltane when the moon was serendipitously waning, which represented the waning of their resistance. As the wax melted onto the pentacle, I imagined them embracing the essence they had previously resisted, becoming as pliant as warm wax in its presence.

This visualization has been related in the first person as a direct example because the more subjective the spell, the better. Try to use whatever you feel to be apt—if someone is giving you a hard time because they are jealous of you, try burning a small green candle to diminish their venom; if the harassment is racial, use a symbol of your culture or background to embed in the melting wax of their waning hostility. An obvious psychological approach is to maintain a friendly, cheerful front: they will try to undermine it, but eventually your courage will be respected, if not liked.

The results of this three-day visualization were as encouraging as they were dramatic. On the first day, one of the major antagonists announced that she was leaving, and became the focus of attention in lieu of me. Her close friend then had a crisis at the idea of being left on her own and hastily endeavored to make other friends—she began to include me. My boss suddenly decided to talk to me about a visit she had made to a psychic, and about bizarre dreams she was having, leading to many enjoyable conversations. By the third day almost everyone was talking to me about UFOs, ghosts, witchcraft, and other subjects; a sure sign of the presence of Hecate in our midst.

Nor did their enthusiasm diminish. By the time I left in November, I had many friends in this unlikely quarter. Our differences became irrelevant and we found common ground not reliant on social or intellectual similarities. Hecate had toppled the petty hierarchy and provided a situation in which mutual tolerance was of benefit to all.

MUNDANE ARCHETYPES

Hecate is rarely found in her entirety in the young, but those with Perse-phone, Artemis, or Isis traits may exhibit aspects of the crone. In older men and women she manifests at midlife, though the Hecate persona often brings with it the conviction that it has always been present. The ensuing occult interest and preoccupation may be difficult for others to handle or understand, but seems totally natural to the person experienc-ing it. In their newfound enthusiasm and, indeed, ability, they are likely to become carried away, possibly in a manner quite unpalatable to oth-ers. This could range from knowing looks, mysterious statements, and deliberately spooky behavior, to outright declarations of psychism and power over others, with the entailing arrogance and tendency to engen-der enemies.

Despite these somewhat dubious traits, Hecate has many positive characteristics, including her often charming eccentricity, which can be light relief in this spiritually depleted era.

She is blessed with genuine healing abilities, which are often expressed early in life within a nursing, midwifery, or psychiatric frame-work. She is a great friend of animals, especially dogs and mogs (a witch's feline), and a source of support to the dying and bereaved. Hecate's per-sonal strength is immense; she acts as if she is immune to the enmity she inevitably attracts.

The Hecate persona can be deeply unpleasant to her enemies, target-ing their weaknesses and lacerating the offensive being with words and curses. She is a Gypsy Rose Lee—her stare full of import beneath her glittering headdress. However, she rarely takes her troubles home with her, and is expert in the self-purification department.

Hecate tends to be physically strong when manifesting in a woman; in men she inhabits the pale, high-strung frame of the "sensitive." The lat-ter will be a sexual failure, possibly still clinging to the apron strings at fifty; in women, one who has chosen to be alone, or who is in control of her own sexuality. In both, she may exhibit trickster qualities.

Hecate has a tendency, like Persephone, to take herself too seriously. However, it is true that she has genuinely seen a lot. The mundane Hecate-archetype usually has a deep personal grievance, possibly from youth, that still pains her: the persona is often used as a mask for a much less confident inner self. She has a love of theater, opera, and dance, and is often physically active (in women).

Her literary skills may be limited to spells, but she loves a good persona. Glamorous actresses with strong personalities, and effeminate, successful men will attract her, along with, of course, the gullible innocents awestruck by her power. She may, however, turn the wheel of fortune quite genuinely in their favor. This is what she always promises, and often delivers.

TAROT CARDS

The Moon, The High Priestess, The Wheel of Fortune.

APHRODITE

She hypnotizes, like the sea.

Waves of euphoria inebriate the senses when she is near; I stand on a rocky outcrop of reason, watching, the vertiginous impulse compelling me to jump. To be consumed in a rapture of water, drowned in the salty brew that looks pure but promises not to be.

Desiring amnesia, my impulses refuse analysis. I feel myself being drawn further into her enchantment, colluding; will under glamour. Ambrosia is offered from a golden chalice, and I drink it greedily. Languor settles on the brain like an eternity of silken sheets.

She performs her part with éclat, feeding off my balmy smile. I am as helpless as a love-stricken adolescent. She lets me paddle in her essence, then withdraws the tide; but I will get her and haul her inland.

Later, she will lie on her back on the fallow furrows, her eyes sky-blue and reflective, her face a golden glow—haughty yet vulnerable; an invitation to be conquered. I will plow her into the earth, commit her life-blood to the soil, and attempt to immobilize her so she does not do this to me again. She always will, of course.

I cannot believe I think this way when she is near. And yet she makes me. She knows what she is doing. Or does she?

She notices me brooding and brings her scent a little closer. Touches me. I forget I ever had a thought.

THE NATURE OF APHRODITE AND HER PRACTICAL APPLICATIONS

According to Hesiod, Aphrodite is created when Uranus' castrated genitals are cast into the sea. Just as Athene's birth from Zeus' head affirms her mental prowess, Aphrodite's creation from sea-frothing genitalia reveals her as the embodiment of sexual desire.

As such, she is a deity of unrivalled popularity. As the legend of Paris' judgment amply demonstrates, the gifts of Artemis (independence, hunting skills, athleticism) and Hera (power, glory, prestige) can barely compete. Indeed, all other goddesses fade in comparison to this epitome of human and celestial desire.

When a person is *in aphrodite*, entranced by love or lust, reason is unlikely to prevail. Moreover, those who attempt to avoid Aphrodite and refuse her gifts do so at their own peril. Hippolytus, for example, dedicated himself to Artemis and scorned Aphrodite; the latter caused his stepmother Phaedra to fall in love with him. Unable to bear rejection, Phaedra then accused him of rape. The long chain of revenge did not end until Hippolytus was dead and the family horribly shamed. The message is clear: to deny the flow of one's libido, personified by Aphrodite, is to court disaster.

It is, therefore, fitting that the Minotaur, symbolic of sexuality so suppressed that it has become a raging subconscious beast, should be a tool of her vengeances. Incest and bestiality are among the punishments inflicted by Aphrodite on those who skimp on the natural outlets of their sexuality and, thereby, refuse to do her homage.

Surprising traits indeed to find in one of such pleasing looks and blessed with such a golden aura. Yet it is Aphrodite's dynamism, both in its positive and negative aspects, that saves her from the category of two-dimensional ornamentation. She is as beneficent as she is malicious, as intense as she is fickle, as physically and spiritually beautiful as she is sickening. Aphrodite brings the affliction of love, the wound whose fevered visions are its own redemption; for only by living through it can the victim, probably willing but a victim nonetheless, really be cured.

These apparent contradictions have produced one of the most enduring of ancient goddesses, an archetype and name instantly recognizable to the modern world. It is typical of the ancient Greek mindset that Aphrodite is not like, say, Lilith in Judeo-Christian mythology, defamed for her powerful sexuality; Aphrodite emerges as a dualistic being with good and bad points, just like the human psyche itself.

Aphrodite is out to get what she can while she can, and her archetype is present in many women today. Having witnessed the abominable abuse of the chthonic form of femininity that predated her, she has become the teenage daughter with all of the power and none of the generosity of her mother. Her role as fertility goddess remains, however, but in a new form. Aphrodite's ability to engender growth resembles that of a solar deity in lieu of the comfortable earth mother, a comparison underlined by her popular epithet "the Golden," and by her association with birds and empyrean qualities. She brings about sexual feeling of all types, not just procreative. Her worshippers are free to revel in amorous sensations of any mutually consensual nature. Aphrodite is a lover, and the works of ancients such as Catullus and Sappho do her appropriate homage. Aphrodite's sexuality has become her own rather than a free-for-all, but she maintains the ability to stimulate proliferation in plants, animals, humans and, indeed, gods. As a Muse, she is unrivalled.

On a psychological level, Aphrodite offers to break the mold of mundane existence and shake the foundations of her lovers with a sublime as well as physical passion. "It is better to have loved and lost . . . " is a motto the goddess herself might well have written.

It is appropriate that the goddess of love is frequently coupled with Ares, the god of war. Just as earth itself spins between the planets Venus and Mars, the terrestrial condition is one of suspension between love and enmity, the two most powerful instincts that pull us here and there according to personal proclivities and the influence exerted by each. Thus, of the four children born to Aphrodite by Ares, two are positive: Eros, meaning love, and Anteros, meaning reciprocal love; and two negative: Daimos, or terror, and Phobos, meaning fear.

Aphrodite can bring either sublimation or tragedy. The story of Helen of Troy is perhaps her best known act of destruction through vanity, in which love and reciprocal love swiftly become enmity and war. Eris, or discord, is rarely far behind her scented train.

Aphrodite is a deity of pronounced social sensibilities, more a fan of courtly love than outright sexuality. She endorses physical passion if it is appropriately timed and stylishly conducted, but crudeness offends her; she is, after all, companion and origin of the lovely Graces, deities worthy of any Jane Austen novel. Imagine her horror at parenting Priapus, a boy whose phallus was so large that she sent him away to the countryside to be forgotten about, she hoped. Priapus is, of course, symbolic of the extremes Aphrodite can provoke. She is designed as the female counterpart to the lusty horned god, but shirks the task. In her independence Aphrodite has been civilized. She has formed herself out of the rudimentary clay of her mother into a predatory, self-sufficient entity with complete autonomy. A bludgeon-like phallus is both distasteful and dangerous to her.

This need to dominate underlies the deceptive frivolity of her "bubbly" nature. She may be as apt to change with the tides as the foam itself, but it is not through lack of intelligence or giddiness that this is so. Aphrodite follows her own desires wherever they may lead, and her hedonism is as relentless as her ire when roused. Cross her, or even bore her, and you've had it. It is thanks to this tenacity that Aphrodite may be approached for purposes not merely superficial. Relationships blessed by Aphrodite will prove physically as well as psychologically passionate, and metaphorically or literally fertile.

As for finding new partners, few deities could offer a more interesting chase. Seduction is Aphrodite's forte; she is the ultimate witch when it comes to love-spells. She does not flinch when the cerebral becomes physical; Aphrodite is a prime role model for the female libido at its most active. Consequently, for claiming or reclaiming one's independent sexuality, Aphrodite is a supremely suitable godform to invoke.

One word of warning: this deity can have serious repercussions on your life. She will invest you with the power to break hearts and ruin as well as create relationships. Other goddesses such as Hathor, Isis, and Iris may be employed to counterbalance her influence, providing the groundwork for a more permanent state of affairs.

APPROACHING APHRODITE: PREPARATION

Try to work with a waxing moon, preferably full.

An indulgent ritual bath is highly recommended prior to any activity involving Aphrodite or her qualities.

The candles should be red, dark orange, and pink. Put lots of bubble bath in the water to recall Aphrodite's emergence from the frothing ocean. The best scents to use are rose, musks, sandalwood, or any perfume that is an erotic stimulant to you.

If you desire, drink wine or ambrosia in the bath; both are appropriate to Aphrodite; however, ambrosia is difficult to acquire unless you brew your own.

If you wish to burn incense or oil, the scents mentioned above are suitable, as are myrrh or cinnamon. Cypress is also sacred to Aphrodite, but may smell a little medicinal for the purpose.

While lolling in the scented waters, imagine that this bath is the preliminary to a much-anticipated date. You are preparing to meet someone you really want to impress. If you are already in a relationship, concentrate on the feelings you had when you first met your partner; if not, envision your ideal counterpart.

Either way, contemplate the newness of their unexplored mind and body, the qualities that attract you to them, and what they will be like to kiss. Think about how smitten they will be by you, and how alluring you will be.

Music often helps with fantasies of this ilk; play something upbeat that makes you feel good, or anything that has, for you, suitable connotations.

As you lie in the warm scented water, concentrate on the chakra that lies at the base of the spine at the genitals, and on the one above it at the spleen. Envision the root chakra growing and glowing in red, and the one above it a mini-sunwheel of vibrant orange. Do this until you can feel a powerful energy flowing between the two. Be aware of the combination of these forces quickening your blood with anticipation and confidence.

With your potential encounter still in mind, perform all the mini-rituals you would before any important date; wash your hair or shave your legs if you are so inclined; you may want to use a nicely scented moisturizer afterward.

Once you have completed your toilette, having applied any make-up and perfume you wish to wear, and are feeling alluring, you are ready to invoke Aphrodite.

VISUALIZATION FOR FINDING YOUR IDEAL SEXUAL PARTNER

First, perform the preparations described above.

Now, make a list of the qualities of your desired partner. Think of the physical traits you find attractive—approximate height, weight, or hair-color, for example—and, most importantly, the character traits you wish for in a partner. Will they be gentle? Assertive? Artistic? Homely? Adventurous? Write each of your specifications on an individual scrap of paper.

If you are not sure what form your ideal partner will take, all the better. The fewer specifications you send out, the wider the range of "applicants." You probably have a sense of the essence of your ideal counterpart, so concentrate on that if their qualities seem indefinable.

Once you have prepared your list, take a small red candle, preferably one that is red throughout instead of painted on the outside, and dip your fingers into a little scented oil such as orange, ylang-ylang, opium, or rosemary—choose a scent that feels right to you.

Hold the candle at the center and place it on a piece of red or black silk; rub your fingers simultaneously on both ends of the stick so half is stroked only from the center to the wick, and half from the center to the base.

As you do this, visualize the type of person you desire being irresistibly magnetized toward you. Feel yourself surrounded by Aphrodite's golden glow, infinitely attractive to those of your choosing, and sense the approach of your desired partner. You are, in effect, "magnetizing" the candle, which will echo and magnify your call in the ether. As you rub, continue to feel the conviction within yourself that, as the candle burns, your request will indeed be transmitted into the etheric airwaves. Try to invest all your excitement into the candle wax.

Make sure you have your paper snippets in your hand; ask for Aphrodite's blessing, and light the candle. As the wick lends itself to the flame, know that your request has been received on the astral plane.

Envision Aphrodite standing in a golden haze just behind the candle flame. She is the living epitome of all that you deem attractive, and the power of allurement emanates from her in compelling golden waves.

Watch the flame signalling your sexual desire, and feel free to day-dream about how wonderful it will be when you experience the result. Mentally collude with Aphrodite as if she were your best friend, sharing your secrets and giggling with you over your schemes.

When you feel ready, pick the quality you consider primary and com-mit it to the flame (best to use tweezers); ensure that the message it con-tains gets through. As it burns, watch Aphrodite receive it on the other side of the candle; she takes the specifications of your special order. Shimmering and smiling, she nods her acquiescence.

Continue in this process until all the qualities you require in your part-ner-to-be have been reconfirmed by you and burned and assimilated by the goddess.

When all have gone, extinguish the candle.

Repeat this process at the same time every day until the candle has burned down. If this is not possible and you feel your request is already bound to be granted, allow the red candle to burn down before you put it out. Do not, of course, leave it unattended.

Now, wait and see who you've conjured.

Most importantly, enjoy yourself and your love-goddess aspect.

RESTIMULATING THE SEX DRIVE

Many people, especially women, find that their libido all but deserts them at some point or another. This can be due to stress, diet, spiritual concerns, or simply boredom. It is very common for women to go off sex once a relationship has been established: Aphrodite deserts them and a more homely deity steps in.

The following visualization is for women who wish to realign them-selves with the sex goddess, not for someone else's sake, but because they miss the sensual dimension in their lives. Others may prefer to remain unsexual; there is nothing wrong with this. Energies used in sexual interaction are often rerouted and used for other equally important purposes. This visualization will help you route the energies back into your sexuality, should you wish to employ them there.

VISUALIZATION FOR RESTIMULATING THE SEX DRIVE

Having performed the preparations described earlier, stand naked before a full-length mirror. If it is too cold or you are uncomfortable, dress in something you like that makes you feel attractive.

Now, imagine your entire body glowing golden: a gentle, warm effulgence that radiates from your mind and your heart. As you do this, half-close your eyes and take several slow, deep breaths. As you breathe with your eyes half-shut, visualize the goddess Aphrodite descending in a golden cloud right behind you. Her cloud merges with yours, and as it does, you feel a physical pleasure permeating your skin, along with a knowledge, once understood but long-forgotten, that your body is your playground.

Notice that Aphrodite wears a girdle around her waist. A large amount of sexual energy is concentrated in this golden girdle: it is the ultimate saucy lingerie. This is the girdle that Aphrodite lent to Hera to seduce her disinterested husband Zeus—it never fails. Ask Aphrodite if you may borrow it.

Now, take a generous amount of the light that flows freely around the goddess and spin it into your lower chakras. If you perceive any cracks or blocks in these areas, heal the rifts and unclog the chakras; ground any unclean matter by throwing it at the floor, or flicking it off with your fingers. It is best to physically enact these processes.

When they are bright and feel fully stimulated and strong, the lower and intestinal chakras a vivid red and orange color, you can stop. Do not quit until these parts of your body feel pleasantly charged with bright energy.

When you feel sated, put one hand on the top of your head and the other on your pubic area. This will even out the energies. Then, for just a moment longer, return to charging your two lowest chakras.

When they are bright and feel fully stimulated and strong, thank Aphrodite and bid her farewell, knowing that a part of her remains with you.

Return to normal, repeating the exercise as often as you wish.

Did Aphrodite give you the girdle? If so, the auspices are good for your libido. Be sure to visualize it around your waist when you are in your next sexual scenario.

If she denied you this ultimate aphrodisiac, repeat the exercise until she acquiesces.

Either way, remember that if you borrow that golden glow for long enough, it will eventually become a part of you.

Mundane Archetypes

Aphrodite is so omnipresent that she is almost impossible to define. She is wherever there is sexual desire and, more importantly, where there is the will to evoke it. She is rampant in teenage girls, prostitutes, and transvestites; self-parody does not offend her, as long as it is sexually effective. Brutish physicality, on the other hand, does.

Aphrodite is every woman or feminine person who dresses to kill. She is the power of seduction, of will over flesh. She is the experimental part of our psyches, the bisexual urge, the part entranced by lust and determined to return the feeling.

Because of her strong focus on her individual power, she can be despotic and merciless, particularly toward other attractive women.

American soap operas have the corner on the kind of low-minded catti-ness such classically attractive women can sink to, all, of course, being fair in love and war.

She likes to consider herself dangerous but can easily endanger her-self by underdressing and flirting excessively. Many Aphrodites wear tiny skirts and revealing tops, but become genuinely offended when men in the street start acting rough.

She is sociologically insolent, relying on civilization to come between her and the nature of the beast. She deliberately invokes a strong sexual response, but it is imperative to her to retain control. Despite her ideo-logical arguments for total sartorial liberation, it is clear that Aphrodite could not survive without the laws of the realm protecting her.

Aphrodite is the commercial world's favorite trick, appearing on countless advertisements for cars, bras, beer, and magazines. Not only is she used to lure others, but her own expensive and ever-changing tastes are comprehensively manipulated by industries such as teeny-bop pop and high street fashion. Suffice to say, Aphrodite is a deeply familiar figure and not quite the feminist ideal she sometimes cracks herself up to be.

TAROT CARDS
The Lovers, The Devil, Ace of Cups.

IRIS

The Harpies and Iris shared a childhood nest; and so light grew up in conjunction with scheming darkness. Triple-headed monsters haunted the pale child day and night, making deformity familiar to her; a matter of no consequence.

Now, free to wander the world, she journeys between dimensions shedding color and understanding in her wake.

Seven iridescent rays provide her bridge; she slides through spectrums of glimmering light. She is fluent in the vibration of each, becoming part of any wavelength and disguising herself as a reflected raindrop, if the gods so will.

She appears aureoled on the lashes of the lamenting, messages of hope her charge, or sometimes those of resignation. Through Iris' intercession,

Demeter was commanded to stoicism over the rape of her daughter. The task, though thankless, was necessary; men perished while the corn goddess mourned. Iris cannot stand by and witness such imbalance.

And so Iris' life is defined as pronouncer of the will of the gods. She listens, she travels, and she tells. Sometimes, she mediates of her own volition. For her soul's palette is extensive, made up of black and white and everything between, and she knows the necessity of all.

Habitually, she emanates an arc between extremes, manifesting as the rainbow.

THE NATURE OF IRIS AND HER PRACTICAL APPLICATIONS

Iris' lesson is similar to Persephone's, in that we see how balance is necessary in all things, as is acceptance of change. In the *Mythic Tarot*, Iris is depicted as Temperance, a symbol of self-control even during times of fluctuation. The angel of Temperance is the oversoul, anchored by spiritual insight in the ever-changing ocean of physical circumstance. Like Iris, the oversoul exhibits gentle optimism and quiet faith in ultimate good.

Iris is employed as Hera's handmaiden and guardian of clouds and rain. However, her chief function is as intermediary. Along with Hermes, Iris is a messenger of the gods. Travelling by the arc of her rainbow she bridges the worlds. It is Iris who is sent by Hera to the soporific chambers of Somnus, the god of sleep, to request that dream-visions be sent to certain devoted mortals. Through Iris' intercessions, Somnus' son, Morpheus, makes known Ceyx's death to his pining wife, Halcyone. Likewise, in *The Iliad*, Zeus employs Iris as swift dispatcher of urgent messages; a verbal stauncher of blood on the battlefield.

Iris travels with ease between kingdoms and dimensions, using her flexible nature to prevent unnecessary suffering. When a mortal is undergoing a slow death, Iris brings relief by severing the silver cord that binds them to this realm. She is a deity of great charity and diplomacy, the antithesis of her sisters, the pestilential Harpies.

When the symbolic champions of spirit, the Boreades, are threatened by the Harpies, Iris is put on the spot. Her positive nature dictates the protection of the Boreades, while her genetic nature does not wish for harm to befall her sisters. Those in the dark corner are fighting furiously but slipping under, their poisonous spittle flying in the wind as they shriek and curse. It seems that both parties might come to a sticky end unless Iris compromises her direful sisters by rescuing them. Finally, she corners them into a deal whereby they leave the Boreades and their hapless charge, King Phineus, in peace.

Thus, Iris mediates between the poles of good and evil, engendering balance amid struggle. Her flexibility and calm in situations that are often dangerous to the outsider are qualities worthy of emulation. It is also interesting that such an active goddess arrests action and, thereby, creates harmony.

She is not a mere follower and deliverer of others' instructions, but an intelligent and kindly judge in her own right. Iris' overriding qualities are gentle strength and communication skills borne of the art of balance.

As the soft hues of her spectrum suggest, Iris is a bringer of hope and justice through diplomacy rather than force. Her temperate nature and ability to adapt to a variety of environments, her easy transition between the realms of material life, sleep, and immortality, and her equipoise in matters sacred and profane make Iris a perfect example of spiritual integrity at its most temperate and tactile. She displays the calm intelligent equilibrium we are urged to attain in such tracts as the *Bhagavad-Gita*; or, in less specific terms, an angelic overview.

Iris is a guide and a herald, conversant in matters practical as well as spiritual. She is an extremely functional goddess; indeed, without verbs defining her, she would be nothing but a pretty rainbow. Instead, she is a bearer of peace to the soul tortured by time and its dead-end facade; her light illuminates the eternity behind it.

Contacting Iris: Preparation

Showering by daylight is a good preliminary to contacting the Iris archetype, preferably with a crystal in the window sending shards of spectrum-light about the room.

Flowers in bud, snowdrops, and the symbols of early spring befit this goddess; but no need to become sickly. Iris is kind and beautiful, but being conversant in all levels of consciousness, keeps at least one end of her rainbow planted firmly on the ground.

For those with ethereal proclivities, place a pot of soil in the room to rub in your hands if you feel yourself becoming too carried away, or simply stamp on the floor, which should help to ground you; or you can make that shower cold.

Initially, you will want to focus on the throat and heart chakras. This will focus the willpower and attune it with emotional intelligence and communication skills.

Turquoise is a color of spiritual compulsion and self-protection. When the green heart and blue throat chakras are combined, one is likely to view life from a spiritual standpoint, allowing intuitive personal development to dominate mundane concerns, including job and relationship matters (particularly if they are unfulfilling).

By employing these chakras and being aware of the colors created, we access the blue vibration of will and the yellow of compassionate love, which abide together in the form of the green heart chakra. This, of course, is a vernal color appropriate to Iris, a goddess of hope and new life, particularly of light after darkness.

Iris is a functional archetype quick to be of use to gods and humanity alike. In invoking (or convoking) her, we may access the more humanitarian and self-disciplined traits of the human psyche. As Iris is simple and straightforward, so is our means of accessing her.

VISUALIZATION FOR INCREASED COMMUNICATION SKILLS

After you have showered and meditated for a while (five minutes should do) on your throat and heart chakras, combine them and surround yourself with green and turquoise light; refresh yourself with a little spring or mineral water, and envision your entire body glowing white. At its center, from the tailbone up to the top of your skull, is an elongated spectrum of red, orange, yellow, green, blue, purple, and violety white. Hold this vision along with a sense of your causal purity.

Now envision the goddess of the rainbow in her robes of white, swift-footed as she casts her arc of gentle all-healing light across the sky. One by one, transfer each color of her rainbow into the relevant power-point along your spine, neck, and skull; as you do, concentrate on the qualities engendered by this benefactress, as follows:

Base chakra: Envision this root area bathed in a powerful red light. Feel the health and vitality of your being, the cleanliness of your blood as it circulates, and your ability to interact with others as the driver of a healthy, active human vehicle. Resolve to do your best by this, and to grasp the moment while you can.

Intestinal chakra: While you contemplate the orange ray and spin it in with your own orange chakra, concentrate on your charisma and ability to get on with others from all walks of life and at all levels of experience. Also, be aware of your faculty of discrimination.

Solar Plexus chakra: Concentrate on the pure compassionate ghee-colored light emanating from the center of Iris' rainbow and connect it with the center of your spinal column, just beneath the base of the sternum. Think of your positive points as a person, and consider how good a friend you are.

If you have hang-ups or doubts in this department, now is the time to clear out your negative feelings to make way for the new, positive approach. Focus bright yellow light on this chakra and send it energy until you feel socially confident and aware of your integrity as a companion and friend.

Selfishness should be consciously eliminated from your criteria in attracting and sustaining friendships; it is not a person's position or physical manifestation that counts, but the essence of their interaction with you. This may sound obvious, but it is surprising how many habitual liaisons, considered to be friendships, are essentially corrupt once the surface is scratched. Purifying the solar plexus chakra will help purge your life of such negative influences. If you are unsure of somebody's motives in wishing to spend time with you, imagine them attached to your solar plexus by a cord (as, indeed, they are), and send bright yellow and white energy into it for as long as you feel inclined.

The state of the cord when you first imagined it will speak volumes. If it was golden, strong, or straightforward, fine; but if frayed, dirty, or otherwise unpleasant-looking, you can imagine the sort of influences it is channeling. Also, its reaction to the positive energy you sent it will tell you a great deal, while simultaneously influencing the relationship in real terms on the astral plane. If it absorbed the light and appeared healthy afterward, you may deduce that your own positive qualities can maintain or even redeem the relationship; if it reacted badly to the light—in the worst case scenario it actually dissolved—you may conclude a case of good riddance to bad rubbish.

Cleansing yourself of negative and vampiristic influences can only help improve your balance and aid the maintenance of a healthy core of inner energy. A cleansing fireball of yellow light will help achieve this goal.

Heart chakra: The color of growth and abundance permeates your heart, inviting new emotional interactions and the flourishing of affections. Consider the integrity of your emotions, your ability, like Iris', to distinguish between affections received or imposed, and those that comprise a genuine response to beings of a higher nature or those spiritually resonant to you.

In addition, imagine a center of white light in this area, indicative of your physical health. Visualize it glowing brilliantly in conjunction with the vibrant green of your heart chakra.

Throat chakra: As you envision this spinning sky-blue discus, imagine lines of thin blue light entering and exiting your throat. These are communication cords, vibrating with the sagacious guidance of your particular spiritual gurus and protectors. Everybody has spirit guides, though some are more evident than others. It is mainly through the throat chakra that they access our systems and make their voices audible to us.

So, as you soak up the blue of Iris' rainbow and incorporate it into your shining astral aura, bear in mind that you are servicing your capacity to receive higher information and, consequently, should find it easier in the future. Of course, the more care you lavish on your psychic radio, the more efficiently it will work and the easier it will be to transmit from it. By concentrating sky-blue light into your throat area, you are improving your fluency in the divine language, not to mention your ability to translate and speak it. This is a good way to cut the nonsense from your dialogue; you will soon find yourself saying only what you mean, and avoiding what you don't.

Third Eye chakra: As you incorporate the final violet streak of Iris' rainbow-light into your system, it causes your forehead to glow a bright purple; resolve to balance your spiritual side with your physical condition on a day-to-day basis. Iris, as Temperance, represents the reconciliation of all elements of being; like her, you will not forget one in deference to another.

Imagine brilliant white light flowing in through your crown chakra and running down your spine via your third eye area. As it hits each glowing color zone it intensifies the light. The tip of your skull becomes white, your forehead vibrates violet, your neck is an airy sky-blue, your heart is a brilliant green, your solar plexus glows like sunlight, your stomach is bright orange, and your base chakra a startling red. The light flows down and up, balancing and replenishing your energy in every extreme of your body. Let it fill outward until it touches the tips of your fingers and flows from your toes, nothing lost; your energy is seemingly limitless. Your astral body is awake now. Feel the balance; the calm knowledge that this is how you should be; this is your original and pure state. Your history means nothing; you are fully empowered to enter your future with confidence in your own abilities and diplomatic skills.

Repeat this exercise whenever you feel in need of a spiritual refresher, or when you simply wish to reharmonize your life with your environments: physical, mental, and spiritual.

Mundane Archetypes

Iris represents more of a function than a personality and, as such, she does not have a mundane archetype. However, anybody exhibiting strong diplomatic abilities and multicultural fluency, along with excellent communication skills and emotional intelligence, is portraying Iris traits . . . when they are in the process of putting them to good use.

Tarot Cards
Temperance, Page of Swords.

GLOSSARY

Amrita: A celestial potion; the Hindu equivalent of ancient Grecian ambrosia. This sweet drink could confer immortality, and was the cause of many struggles between gods, devas, and asuras—the angels and demons of Hindu mythology.

Astral Body: In Western terms, the third body (after the physical and subtle) relating to emotion, dreams, and creative inspiration. It is usually the vehicle for astral travel.

Akasha: The fifth element after air, earth, fire, and water; represented in the West as the tip and surrounding circle of the pentacle. In the East it usually takes the form of a purple or black egg, symbol of all knowledge. Relates to the upper three *chakras*.

Beltane: May Day, the most fertile and green of the *Sabbats*. A powerful and positive current in the Western hemisphere.

Bindi: Mark traditionally placed on the foreheads of Hindu women to denote marriage or religious adherence.

Casting a Circle: A circle is cast before magickal rites by invoking the *Quarters* in turn, each of which represents a particular element and point of the compass. The caster traces the circle in the air or on the ground and strongly envisions this area blessed and protected by the elements and free of negative influence. Once it is cast, the circle becomes a sphere of protection and anonymity (if desired) in which magickians can then freely perform their activities. It is sometimes helpful to cast a circle prior to a tarot reading or visualization: it also serves to focus one's attention and to enhance psychic perceptions. At the end of the activity, the circle can either be deconstructed or left to fade on its own, though it is not usually passed through while still in operation. See *Quarters, invoking* for further details.

Causal Body: The finest of the body-sheaths, relating to the highest principles of individual and cosmic existence.

Chakra: Focal points on the body; variously described as wheels, whirlpools, and discs of light, these centers distribute life-energy throughout the psycho-spiritual and physical systems. They are used in many yogic techniques, and can be utilized in visualization and magick as keys to specific traits and aspects of the self, as well as to engender particular energy-levels. The seven major chakras are detailed in the Introduction.

Dharma: The Sanskrit name for the principle of cosmic order. The code of conduct of the individual that safeguards integrity and ensures longevity of the soul. Virtue and the upholding of sacred law. In Nature, the balance and sustenance of the Universe.

Etheric Body: In Western terms, the layer of aura between the physical body and the *astral*.

Ghee: Clarified butter popular in India; often of a particularly rich, yellow color. It is used as a smearing-substance during the festival of Holi, a street-and-temple carnival in which paint-powder is liberally thrown at all in the vicinity.

Gitagovinda: A twelfth-century tract depicting the story of Krishna and Radha in the form of a pastoral play.

Higher Self: The sure, still voice within; the part of the constitution not influenced by mundane concerns and ephemeral emotions. The overseer of incarnations; the wise guardian of the individual; this is the part of us most conversant with cosmic energies, and of the most use when approaching deities and the like. One interpretation is that the Higher Self is the part of the soul it is most easy to communicate with; another is that it is the archetypal expression of one's essence, garnered during countless modes of being; a psycho-spiritual "mean average." It is not a manifestation of the singular subconscious; it is both coherently accessible and independent of the body, though it helps to fashion the physical self and its attributes. However, the definition is by nature subjective, and there are probably as many forms of Higher Self as there are individuals on this earth. In this book, the term is used to indicate the spirit-self with which it is possible to communicate, and the side of us that represents the sum of our wisdom, insight, and clarity of vision.

Kali Yuga: In Hindu philosophy, the present age; the last of four whose traits have degenerated as they progressed. Ours is an era of strife, ignorance, and discord; in which mantric meditation is purported to be the chief path to redemption. The Krishna mantra, or "maha-mantra," is said to counteract the effects of the *Kali Yuga* when chanted.

Kama: Hindu god of love; equivalent to Grecian Eros/Cupid. Also, the qualities of desire, love, and pleasure; along with wealth and prestige, one of the chief lures of this plane. Kama can be granted by Laksmi, and is the sole pursuit of Radha and Krishna.

Mataji: *Honored Mother*; an Indian term applied to benefactresses of all kinds, including divine.

Matrikas: *Little Mothers*; the seven gruesome clones of Kali and/or Durga who help them in battle.

Moksa: In Hinduism, *beauty*; a gift bestowed by such beneficent deities as Laksmi; also, liberation from mundane existence.

Paramahansa: Literally, *supreme swan*; the title given to elevated spiritual masters (such as Paramahansa Yogananda) with reference to their transcending of earthly matters. Like the swan, they glide on the murky waters of this realm, their whiteness, or purity, undefiled. Also, a celestial swan used as a mount by such deities as Laksmi and Sarasvati.

Prana: The "breath" of life; sometimes visible as fast-moving globules of energy; usually construed as yellow in color. This energy can be consciously assimilated into the body, particularly through visualization and breathing techniques. There are several different types of *prana*, including the cosmic and five physical varieties.

Prema: Selfless love, as exemplified by Radha in her most positive aspects.

Puja: Meaning *worship*. In India, the celebration or festival of a particular deity, sometimes lasting a number of weeks.

Quarters, invoking: When *casting a circle*, the entities representing the elements are invoked, along with the elements of air, fire, water, and earth themselves. Each of these *Quarters* is stationed at a particular point of the compass, the correspondences being air: east; fire: south; water: west; and earth: north. The magickian provides the fifth element, the *Akashic* principle, and the circle becomes a microcosmic universe in which all matter is contained. The magick or ritual activity is then performed with the Lords of the Elements standing guard against unwanted influences.

Sabbat: There are eight major *Sabbats*, all of them agricultural in origin, and sometimes referred to as the Wheel of Life. They represent crucial points in the tides of the energy of the cosmos, and allow for different modes of magickal work. Sabbats are also celebrated on the full moon, or at the nearest possible time before one. The energy of the Sabbat is usually harnessed and used for specific purposes. The major celebrations are: Imbolc (February 1st), the Spring Equinox (March 21st), Beltane (May 1st), the Summer Solstice (June 21st), Lammas (August 1st), the Autumn Equinox (September 21st), Samhain (October 31st), and the Winter Solstice (December 21st). Many of these Sabbats are celebrated on the eve before, when the energy is particularly strong.

Satya Yuga: In Hindu philosophy, the first of the four ages, the Golden Aeon of Truth and closeness to God—indeed, the opposite of this one. It equates with the Western Atlantean Era.

Samhain: The Celtic celebration of October 31st, when the emphasis is on death and rebirth, cycles of continuity, and the eternity behind the veil of physicality. It is also a time of easy interaction with other planes of existence.

Shakti: In Hindu mythology, a feminine consort and power; the female aspect of the Cosmic Intelligence, embodied by the wife of Siva. An active energy and strength.

Sistrum: A musical instrument that produces a jingling metallic sound, possibly used to ward off evil. It is particularly associated with Hathor and Isis.

Solarization: The process of imprinting a substance such as water with the properties of, say, color or gemstones, by subjecting it to strong sunlight in conjunction with these properties. See Introduction for further details.

Vedas: The scriptures of Hinduism, consisting of the *Rigveda*, or hymns to the gods; the *Samaveda*, or priests' chants; the *Yajurveda*, or magickal prose; and *Arthavaveda*, or mantras and chants. There are many subcategories, of which the Upanishad philosophies are probably the best known. Other texts are also of vast significance, especially the *Bhagavad-Gita*, derived from the *Mahabharata*, the epic poem ascribed to Vyasa.

Vina: A four-stringed Indian instrument not unlike a diminutive sitar; enjoyed by many deities, particularly Sarasvati.

Viraha: Love in separation, such as that evinced by Radha for Krishna.

Vratas: In Hinduism, tasks or penances performed with a particular goal in mind, usually during the festival or in the temple of the deity specific to that goal.

Wicca: The popular form of modern witchcraft; established in differing forms by Gerard Gardener and Alex Sanders in the decades around the 1960s, and now widely spread. This form of nature-worship, combined with magick and individual spirituality, appeals to many whose spiritual lifeblood has been drained by orthodox religions and contemporary modes of living, and who prefer a Goddess-orientated or gender-balanced religion to the more conventional options.

Yantra: The Hindu system of sacred geometry in diagram-form; used in association with a mantra to activate its properties. Yantras, like spells, are designed to cover every conceivable desire, from protection to progeny to spiritual liberation.

BIBLIOGRAPHY

Ashcroft-Nowicki, Dolores. *The New Book of the Dead*. London: Aquarian/Thorsons, 1992.

Atreya: Prana. *The Secret of Yogic Healing*. York Beach, Maine: Samuel Weiser, Inc., 1996.

Beckman, Howard. Mantras, Yantras & Fabulous Gems: *The Healing Secrets of the Ancient Vedas*. Great Britain: Balaji Publishing Co., 1997.

Bernard, Theos. *Hindu Philosophy*. Bombay: Jaico Publishing House, 1989.

Bhaktivedanta, Swami Prabhupada. *Bhagavad-Gita As It Is*. Los Angeles: Bhaktivedanta Book Trust, 1986.

———. *The Perfection of Yoga*. Los Angeles: Bhaktivedanta Book Trust, 1984.

Bonds, Lilian Verner. *Colour Healing*. London: Vermilion, 1997.

Budge, Sir E. A. Wallis. *The Book of the Dead*. London: Routledge & Kegan Paul Ltd., 1956.

Brennan, Barbara Ann. *Hands of Light*. New York: Bantam Books, 1988.

Butler, W. E. *Apprenticed to Magic & Magic and The Qabalah*. London: The Aquarian Press, 1990.

Farrar, Janet and Stewart. *Eight Sabbats for Witches*. Great Britain: Robert Hale, 1984.

Fortune, Dion. *Psychic Self-Defence*. London: Thorsons, 1995.

———. *The Sea Priestess*. Northamptonshire: Aquarian Press, 1989.

———. *Moon Magic*. London: Society of the Inner Light, 1995.

Frazer, Sir James. *The Golden Bough, A Study in Magic and Religion*. Abridged version. Hartfordshire: Wordsworth Editions Ltd., 1993.

Grant, Joan. *Eyes of Horus*. London: Corgi Books, 1975.

———. *Winged Pharaoh*. Ohio: Ariel Press, 1987.

Grant, Kenneth. *Hecate's Fountain*. London: Skoob, 1991.

Graves, Robert. *The White Goddess*. London: Faber and Faber, 1961.

Harrison, Jane. *Themis: A Study of the Social Origins of Greek Religion*. London: Merlin Press Limited, 1963.

Harshananda, Swami. *Hindu Gods and Goddesses*. Madras: Sri Ramakrishna Math, 1987.

Homer. *The Iliad*. Translated by Robert Fitzgerald. Oxford: Oxford University Press, 1984.

Houston, Jean. *The Hero and the Goddess: The Odyssey as Mystery and Initiation*. London: Aquarian/Thorsons, 1992.

Ions, Veronica. *Egyptian Mythology*. Middlesex, England: Paul Hamlyn, 1968.

Kinsley, David. *The Goddess' Mirror: Visions of the Divine from East and West*. Albany, New York: State University of New York Press, 1989.

————. *Hindu Goddesses: Vision of the Divine Feminine in the Hindu Religious Tradition*. Delhi: Motilal Bersidass, 1987.

Knight, Gareth. *The Practice of Ritual Magic*. New Mexico: Sun Chalice Books, 1996.

Larousse. *Larousse Encyclopaedia of Mythology*. Edited by Robert Graves. London: Paul Hamlyn, 1964.

Lemesurier, Peter. *The Healing of the Gods: the Magic of Symbols and the Practise of Theotherapy*. Dorset: Element Books Limited, 1988.

McLeish, Kenneth. *Myth*. London: Bloomsbury, 1996.

Mumford, Dr. Jonn. *A Chakra and Kundalini Workbook*. St. Paul, Minnesota: Llewellyn Publications, 1995.

Paglia, Camille. *Sexual Personae: Art and Decadence from Nefertiti to Emily Dickinson*. New Haven, Connecticut: Yale University Press, 1990.

Prabhavananda, Swami and Christopher Isherwood. *Bhagavad-Gita: Song of God*. Madras: Sri Ramakrishna Math, undated.

Sharman-Burke, Juliet. *The Mythic Tarot Workbook*. London: Rider Books, 1989.

Versluis, Arthur. *The Egyptian Mysteries*. New York: Arkana, 1988.

Vivekananda, Swami. *Hanuman Chalisa*. Madras: Sri Ramakrishna Math, undated.

Wills, Pauline. *Colour Therapy*. Dorset: Element Books Limited, 1993.

Yogananda, Paramahansa. *Autobiography of a Yogi*. California: Self-Realization Fellowship, 1990.

———. *The Divine Romance*. California: Self-Realization Fellowship, 1992.

Zaehner, R. C., editor and translator. *Hindu Scriptures*. London: Everyman, 1992.

INDEX

The Goddess Companion
Daily Meditations on the Feminine Spirit

PATRICIA MONAGHAN

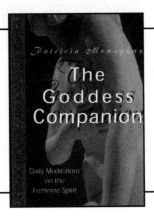

Engage your feminine spirit each day of the year! Here are hundreds of authentic goddess prayers, invocations, chants, and songs—one for each day of the year. They come from dozens of sources, ranging from the great classical European authors Ovid and Horace, to the marvelously passionate Hindu poets Ramprasad and Ramakrishna, to the anonymous gifted poets who first composed the folksongs of Lithuania, West Africa, and Alaska. In fresh, contemporary language that maintains the spirit of the originals, these prayers can be used for personal meditation, for private or public ritual, or for your own creative inspiration. They capture the depth of feeling, the philosophical complexity, and the ecological awareness of goddess cultures the world over.

Organized as a daily meditation book, *The Goddess Companion* is also indexed by culture, goddess, and subject, so you can easily find prayers for specific purposes. Following each prayer is a thoughtfully written piece of prose by Patricia Monaghan which illustrates the aspects of the Goddess working in our everyday lives.

- A perpetual calendar with a daily reading on each page—366 in all
- Includes prayers from Greece, Rome, North and South America, Lithuania, Latvia, Japan, Finland, Scandinavia, India, and many others
- In translations that fully reveal their beauty, making them immediately accessible and emotionally powerful
- Locate goddess prayers by culture, subject, and goddess names

1-56718-463-4
7½ x 9⅛, 312 pp. $17.95

To order, call 1-800-THE MOON
Prices subject to change without notice